STOP
the BLEEDING

Rick Johnson, Ph.D.

Outskirts Press, Inc.
Denver, Colorado

Stop the Bleeding
Surviving Tough Economic Times
All Rights Reserved.
Copyright © 2010 Dr. Rick Johnson, Ph.D.
V3.0

Outskirts Press, Inc.
http://www.outskirtspress.com

ISBN: 978-1-4327-4617-9

Outskirts Press and the "OP" logo are trademarks belonging to Outskirts Press, Inc.

PRINTED IN THE UNITED STATES OF AMERICA

Acknowledgments

Recognition and Appreciation

Publication Support provided by:
Heather Parsons, Author of You Know What I'm Sayin'
Illustrations By: James Harper – guyinzeback@yahoo.com
Cover Design by: David Distefano - distefanodesign@cox.net

Table of Contents

Introduction

Although I know I haven't "seen it all" when it comes to the distribution business, I feel like the more than forty years of experience that I have chalked up (including 10 years as a Business Consultant and Executive Coach) has introduced me to many of the problems you readers may be facing today. This is especially true considering the economic challenges created by these turbulent times. I learned a lot during my career and I continue to learn every day.

"Stop the Bleeding" is not just about managing a Turn-A-Round situation in a failing business or creating contingency plans to deal with economic turbulence. True, I spent ten years of my career involved in several Turn-A-Round situations as well as managing change in a successful rapid growth environment. Additionally, I have faced the challenge of creating a culture shift in profitable but unsuccessful environments. That's a roundabout way of explaining my specific experience as the "Darth Vader of Distribution" during my ten years as a "Turn-A-Round" specialist while protecting the confidentiality of the companies I have been involved with. "Stop the Bleeding" goes beyond the fundamentals of managing a failing business.

This book touches on most of the ingredients that are essential to the survival and growth of the company in the new millennium and provides the methodology for dealing with tough market economics. At this point I must preface my remarks by stating my simple but honest belief as to what is the real key to success. When you discuss your own career, you tend to use a lot of I's. Personally, however, I truly believe the real key to success in any business is "people." Let me repeat that, "People are the key to success in any business."

That may sound like an old human resources cliché, but in reality I have found that if you surround yourself with the right kind of people, you don't have to be a genius. If I were to identify my personal major contributor to my success I would definitely say that it was the ability to pick good people, identify their strengths and weaknesses and ultimately taking advantage of their strengths and negating their weaknesses. Equally as important is the ability to identify your own strengths and weaknesses.

Wolves and Leadership

This book uses many illustrations of the wolf. The wolf was selected as the corporate logo for the my company, CEO Strategist, a consulting firm specializing in strategic leadership development and sales effectiveness, as a symbol of strength in leadership.

SO EXACTLY WHAT DO WOLVES HAVE TO DO WITH LEADERSHIP?

The wolf is a very social animal. Wolves travel together, eat together, hunt together and play together. They are referred to as a pack. The pack is generally a larger family group. Wolves within the pack are related by blood line. Being accepted, respected and cared for by their siblings and parents is important to the wolf. This culture is set by the alpha wolf. *Isn't being cared about, trusted and respected important to every employee of every successful organization in the country? Don't successful leaders promote this type of culture within their organization?*

Just as management hierarchies vary in size, wolf packs vary in size but average five to seven members. *Does that sound like an executive team?* Each pack member plays a specific role with a very specific rank. Some young wolfs go off on their own (Lone Wolves), in search of their status. Generally speaking, the older wolves in the pack tend to be the leaders and they command the respect of the pack. They make the decisions for the group. The pack protects itself and it protects one another.

The lead wolf plays the role just as it sounds. He leads the pack. In fact, they generally will travel in single file with the lead wolf blazing the trail and setting the pace. *Sounds like the role of the CEO doesn't it?*

The lead wolf, however, is not afraid to share his role. He will at times step aside to allow another up and coming wolf to take the lead. Make no mistake; each wolf in the pack has specific responsibilities. Each know in their own right that even if they don't aspire to be lead wolves, they must be prepared to step up to that responsibility if called upon. *Does this have any relationship to bench strength and succession?*

Dominant wolves in the pack that do aspire to be leaders establish themselves in various ways. They might be larger, stronger or simply have a more aggressive personality. Captive wolves have been studied for years indicating complex behavior with regard to governance within the pack. Their communication with one another is also more elaborate than most of the other animal species.

Wolves are very patient of themselves and of one another. They are very focused on their objective whatever it may be at the time. They respect each other's role and depend that each wolf in the pack will live up to their individual responsibility. This in itself promotes group unity. Wolves are very careful that they do not enter into redundant duplicate efforts. Each wolf can be heard by the pack; a form of individual respect. *Could we actually write a corporate mission statement from this paragraph?*

Wolves have a sense of urgency. They depend on one another. They are very focused, hard workers when it comes to feeding themselves. They are one of the wildest most effective hunters and yet in spite of that they hunt to live. They do not live to hunt. They live by an unwritten code that says the good of the pack comes first. *How often do we uncover unsuccessful companies that are unsuccessful because the CEO or ownership put personal needs ahead of business needs?*

Lastly, one of the most common characteristics of the most successful leaders in industry today is the extreme sense of curiosity. Wolves share this incessant curiosity about the world around them. They investigate everything, taking nothing for granted. They seek out opportunity. They have established specific priorities. *Isn't that what successful leaders in business do today starting with the development of a strategic plan?*

The Foundation for Surviving Tough Economic Times

Make no mistake, surviving tough economic times demand effective leadership. This book will touch on all phases of leadership necessary to not only survive tough economic times but to thrive during tough economic times. Just as wolves are courageous and show little fear, effective leaders show no fear as fear causes panic response management which leads to knee jerk reactions and failure.

During my career I saw many changes take place in the industry, but I also experienced some bazaar incidents that may not even sound believable in print. Throughout the content of this book, I hope to not only present you with my views on leading a small to mid-size company to growth and profitability, but I plan to share some of my personal experiences as well.

Change is Inevitable

A great deal of the focus in "Stop the Bleeding" will be spent on leadership, managing change and promoting growth whether it involves a failing company, contingency planning, strategic planning, or even running a successful company that wants to maintain its edge as **Vendor of Choice.**

The principles discussed in this book can be applied universally to any of these situations. The only portion that's unique to the Turn-A-Round situation is the actual tourniquet you apply to "Stop the Bleeding" and the initial restructuring method used to create a new vehicle for success. Of course, when an owner recognizes he has a failing or even a struggling business, there is a tendency to operate on the outer edge of rationalism under a crisis mode short-term management style. This often creates self-inflicted wounds and unusual circumstances both internal and external to the company. That is one of the primary reasons I decided to write this book in an effort to help anyone who find themselves in this situation to get a grip and not to panic. Of course, I would regret it if I didn't emphatically state that my first recommendation would be to seek outside help. So, let's get started. I hope you enjoy the reading.

—**Rick Johnson**

"The Real Deal"

The very first time I faced the reality of "Stopping the Bleeding" was with my own company in 1982. I started BurJon Steel in 1980 when interest rates exceeded twenty percent. Naturally, when you start a business with only $1000 you are instantly highly leveraged. With a $600,000 Small Business Administration (SBA) loan, we began construction on a 15,000 square foot warehouse that would house vintage equipment, a slitter built in 1949 to process steel coils. Unfortunately there were many delays, mostly weather related. We were six months behind schedule for completion of the warehouse. We were supplying slit steel coils to a customer base in the appliance, lawn and garden, and HVAC industry. Since our plant was not complete we were sub-contracting our processing of the steel coils. Being totally debt financed with sales lingering around two million dollars put a heavy burden on cash flow. In fact, we were in a negative cash flow position. We managed to ward off the predators and open up the new plant, processing our own material. Unfortunately, we had dug a pretty deep hole for ourselves. I'll never forget the day our local accountant, a good friend of mine, walked into my office and said:

"Rick, just give it up. You are too far in the hole. The bank is ready to pull the plug. You might want to talk to your attorney about bankruptcy options."

I knew we were struggling, but I still had that lack of fear, that feeling of invincibility and yes, that stupid naivety that comes from youth (I was in my early thirties). My response was very short but not very sweet; it was the slang terminology for "Bovine Fescues" -- -- "Bull Shit!"

The bank did try to pull the plug but we weren't ready to quit. We had a group of employees that believed in what they had created. The bank previously authorized us to mail checks to our suppliers that we had been holding waiting for their approval on an increased cash advance against our line of credit. They gave us that approval verbally but three days later as the checks started to clear we received a call from the bank stating that they would not cover the checks, they would let them bounce. This immediately got our attorney involved. That's when I learned my very first Basic Business Principle, "Self Assessment."

Today we call it a SWOT Analysis

Sounds like something from the TV show "Cops." In reality a SWOT analysis is an effective way of doing a gut check assessment of your business. The acronym SWOT stands for Strengths, Weaknesses, Opportunities and Threats. Done right, with your ego moved to the side, this analysis can make clear the reality of the situation. Although at the time I didn't realize what I was learning, I later realized that the core issue involved in stopping the bleeding is to truly understand the situation that you are in. I mean really understanding by eliminating pride, ego, dysfunctional arrogance and unfounded optimism. So how do you go about developing a SWOT analysis?

1. Strengths

2. Weaknesses
3. Opportunities
4. Threats

Strengths and Weaknesses

Internal analysis by the executive team is essential but you can't rely on that alone. A targeted, selective employee survey balanced with an external vendor/customer survey provides a more accurate picture of the strengths and weaknesses. Always start with your strengths. Dwell on the positives first. Things may not be as bad as you think. Take a realistic view of your company from the outside looking in. Hire an outside pair of eyes to help with the assessment process. Talk to your suppliers, your customers and even your employees. If you belong to a trade association, seek their help. Benchmarking is an excellent way to identify both the strengths and weaknesses of your company. Study "industry par reports" and look at best of the class comparisons from your industry. The following areas may be included both as strengths or weaknesses. In some cases the same issue could be both a strength and a weakness.

- Market Presence
- Brand Recognition or lack of
- Inventory
- ISO Certification System
- Infrastructure
- Distribution Channels
- Marketing programs
- Technical Competence
- Employee Morale ----- Turnover
- Loss or Gain in Market Share
- Recruitment of Personnel
- Seamless Customer Service or lack of

- Logistics Systems
- Vision ----- Strategy
- Finance Issues ----- Capitalization

Opportunities

Opportunities go beyond the ability to gain market share. You need to look into many areas that may have hidden opportunities that you haven't recognized in the past. These are opportunities to not only grow your business but to seek best of the class status. The Japanese have used the term "Kaizen" which means "continuous improvement." Look at areas to improve as opportunities to succeed.

- Employee turnover (opportunity to upgrade)
- E-Commerce
- Product Line Expansion
- New Product Acquisition
- Branding
- Strategic Alliances
- New Markets
- Consolidations
- Centralization
- Restructuring
- Acquisitions
- Divestitures

Threats

Threats can be any number of things. In fact, no matter how comprehensive and speculative you become, each and every company is unique. You should be able to identify many categories not listed in any of the examples.

Don't get the idea that a simple SWOT analysis is going to provide all the answers. It won't. It is nothing more than a tool to help you ask the right questions and look in the right places. One of the basic mistakes most management teams make during their strategic planning process is to just check the box called SWOT analysis. They fail to understand that the real value of this exercise is to recognize and deal with critical constraints that will impede progress; stop you in your tracks. When it comes to a Turn-A-Round situation or even if you just face declining profits and are struggling, you really have to do a gut check analysis of yourself, your management team and your company in its entirety. Get off your duff and find out what's going on inside your company; call in an outside pair of eyes, someone who is willing to look you in the eye and tell you the truth.

In most situations that I have been involved with, the problem has not been caused by the market, the competition, channel strategies, the economy or a poor sales marketing effort. Predominantly I have found that a major portion of the responsibility for the problem lies with upper management. Sure market forces can create difficulties and the economy is certainly a factor. But, effective leadership is absolutely essential to overcome these challenges during economic turbulence. And yes, sometimes it is the President, CEO or owner that has created the problem or in some cases is the problem.

Back to the BurJon story. . .

When we received that phone call in 1982 cutting off all cash flow, we panicked. Was this the end? Was our accountant right? Did we fail? After the dust settled from the fur flying around our attorneys, we quickly updated and revised our business plan which included a Catastrophic, Realistic and Optimistic forecast and a contingency strategy. We went shopping in the finance community. Our plea of "don't give up on us now" along with a commitment we received from a venture capitalist soothed the bank and bought us enough time to recover. One year later we took that bank out. It wasn't easy but we had a good team and the worst was behind us. We had to give up part ownership (20 percent) but it was worth it in the long run. Nine years later, Burjon Steel reached $25 million in revenue and we sold the company to a national service center chain.

The Basics

We were in a Turn-A-Round situation so we went back to the basics. When a company feels the pressures of declining profits, lost market share, increased turnover and low employee morale, these are warning signs that obviously suggest trouble. What are some of the other warning signs?

- Inability to take advantage of discounts
- Pressure from the bank
- Being put on C.O.D. or credit hold by our suppliers
- Credit line at its maximum for extended period
- Receivables aging increased
- Increased ageing of your payables
- Increased inventory and a lower turn rate

Now is the time for gut wrenching reality. What is really wrong with the business? Running a business is not rocket science, but it is amazing how easy we can become all screwed up.

Key Elements

The success of any organization is based upon its ability to manage two key elements (Sales and Margin) in a fundamental way; to not only provide the kind of service to make your company *vendor of choice,* but to also provide an acceptable level of profit in doing so. The third element (Leadership) must also be a top priority. You must be able to lead your people in such a way that their efforts automatically provide success within the first two elements. Finance and operations the final two elements that support profit creation are greatly influenced by the ability to:

1. Raise prices - sell higher
2. Lower - cost
3. Increase efficiencies
4. Create continuous improvement
5. Improve cash to cash cycling -- reduced receivables aging, lower inventory, increased turn rates, extended terms from suppliers

These five factors can only be successful if your people are energized, motivated and empowered to get the job done. Of course they must have a clear understanding of the objectives and vision of the corporation. This requires effective communication throughout the organization. This is so important that we dedicated an entire chapter to it.

"Manage your Assets but Lead your People"

I have had suggestions made to me by owners, presidents and CEOs that would baffle the mind of most professionals that have integrity. For example, I once was asked to fire an individual because his wife's illness had caused the company to reach their catastrophic cap in their insurance program. This same owner would intentionally run mail that contained checks to his vendors through the meter at two cents so they would arrive with postage due. He thought this was a great cost savings idea until the government sent him a cease and desist letter.

I once witnessed an owner make an announcement over the corporate PA system; he announced; "Don't _ _ _ _ with Sally today because 'it's that time of the month' and she'll rip your head off."

Sometimes companies are successful in spite of their personal leadership model. However, failure to treat employees with **respect** is the number one factor leading to failure.

Self Assessment

When you find yourself in the situation where profits are declining and the business is failing you often have to find out things for yourself. A self assessment of your personal leadership model is essential. Who are you? What do you believe in? Do you have a vision? Do you communicate that vision? Do you trust your employees and your executive team? Do you respect them? Don't always believe what you hear and don't always think the problems and solutions are obvious. A CEO once said to me that his only problem was that he had an entire sales force that was incompetent.

Sarcastically, he stated,

"They suffer from Attention Deficit Disorder. We need to fire the majority of them and start from scratch. After all, it's obvious that all we need to do to become profitable is to sell more. My sales force just isn't capable of doing it. If I replace all of them, we can double our sales."

How many times have we heard that simplistic answer?

"We just need to sell more."

Sometimes that statement is true but more often than not it ranks right up there with the ancient salesman's cliché.

"Its low margin business but we'll make it up on volume."

In the case I mentioned, the CEO originally had good vision and a viable strategy. Unfortunately, he failed to not only sell that vision, but he failed to communicate it effectively. Additionally, he failed to recognize the value of his employees. He did not show any respect or trust in their abilities. Creating success with even the best strategy isn't always within your total control. If your people aren't on-board, and they don't respect your ability to lead them, you'll fail. You must lead your people not manage them. Leadership starts with **respect**.

Don't Get Bit by Your Own Rattlesnake

Honest negative feedback is difficult to accept. It takes tremendous courage. I learned that twenty years ago. I thought I knew just about everything there was to know about running a company let alone a smaller 75 million dollar division. I had owned and sold several successful businesses and that success certainly enlarged my ego even

Don't Get Bit by Your Own Rattlesnake!

though I didn't realize it at the time. I was a little too self-indulged and my self confidence bordered on arrogance and stupidity; just like the CEO I quoted that thought his entire sales force was incompetent. I even had a rattlesnake sitting on my desk with a statement that can't be printed exactly as it appeared, due to censorship and morality.

It read……………..

"You'd rather kiss a rattlesnake than _ _ _ _ with me."

Now, that's not exactly a good example of the kind of leadership that I try to promote today. So, if we are going to improve as leaders, we must have the courage to recognize and admit how stupid we can act at times. Courage is one character trait that is a mainstay of every successful leader. Every successful leader I have ever met demonstrated courage and a willingness to accept their own fallacies. They seemed to have a unique ability to honestly listen to negative feedback.

That's easy to say but during the time I boldly displayed my rattlesnake, I didn't have that kind of courage. I had no concept of the image or the message my actions represented. I didn't listen very well to negative feedback. In fact, until the CEO of the company I worked for at the time called it to my attention, I didn't realize that the rattlesnake was just a symptom of many things that were wrong with my personal leadership model.

It was a Wakeup Call

You see, it wasn't long before we had a real issue that the corporate office and I didn't quite see eye to eye on. We didn't agree on how it should be handled. The issue was dealing with the introduction of a union in the operating division that I was running. I wanted to take a strong stance of opposition. Ultimately, within ninety days, we agreed to disagree, I left and they were happy. It was the one time in my career that I can actually say I was fired even though it wasn't presented that way (or maybe it was, but just because of my ego and ignorance I didn't accept it that way). I learned a lot from that experience. At first it was a punch in the stomach, but very soon afterwards I realized that I'd better wake up. This was a turning point for me. I realized that I was still a young man with a lot to learn and a lot to offer. It was that day that I finally got the courage to look into the mirror and reflect on my personal leadership model and my behavior as a person. Sure, I did a lot of things right. I had a lot of leadership qualities. But, I also did a lot of things wrong. I honestly believe that my early success, that was a result of some of those leadership characteristics, actually threw me off track. I knew then that I had to really work on my leadership skills.

I went on from there to become very successful in helping companies maximize their effectiveness. I learned many things on that journey that started 20 years ago and I am still learning today.

Leadership is not easy

That is the first thing I learned. Leadership evolves as conditions change, circumstances change; the people around you change and you change as an individual. Just as I have often said about sales effectiveness – *"There is no Purple Pill."* Rest assured, there is no purple pill that you can take to become an effective leader. Additionally, no matter how much experience you have, common sense is still a major performance indicator. Effective leadership must incorporate common sense to keep you at ground level. Ask yourself, do you have some form of rattlesnake in your leadership model?

Leaders influence people and get them to realize their maximum potential. But, to do that, leaders must be able to recognize and understand themselves. Otherwise, as I did with my rattlesnake, we will not be able to comprehend the appropriate use of the *"Tools of Authority."* Remember, with authority comes responsibility; the responsibility of honesty, trustworthiness and integrity. It's not about being a BOSS!

Understanding the two types of authority

Yes, even though I teach the concepts of servant leadership, authority is still a part of leadership that involves your position in the hierarchy of the organization. Authority that is assumed based on your title is known as formal authority. This type of authority can help you get things done, but it doesn't mean you should strike like the rattlesnake. Utilizing formal authority alone is the old autocratic, lone wolf style of leadership that just isn't acceptable to today's employees. Formal authority, used inappropriately as the only means of management, may get short-term results but it can do long-term damage.

Trust and Respect

Informal authority, authority that is earned out of respect, is the authority granted to you by the employees. It is the authority you have as viewed in the minds and hearts of your employees. It is based on your ability to trust and respect your employees. It means that you recognize that they are your most valuable asset. As a result you earn their trust and their respect for you as a leader.

Speaking of trust and respect, I once worked with an owner of mid-size distributorship with revenue between $50 and $100 million. We were discussing employee issues and the fact that his business had become stagnant. I mentioned employee turn-over and he quickly said he wasn't overly concerned.

In fact he said: *"I have a 'won't leave' list."*

I questioned him regarding this and he opened his top desk drawer and showed me a list with eleven names on it.

"These are people, that no matter what I do --- they won't leave," he said with smirkish pride in his voice.

He continued as he pointed to one of the names. *"Like Suzie here, she has two boys in a day care center that is just a block away from here. She visits them during her lunch hour. It's quite convenient for her. She will never leave. So..... when raise time comes I may only give her 2% as compared to 5% for someone else."*

Not only did he not recognize that what he was doing was illegal, he had no clue of the impact that it had on the entire organization. Once I completed a business assessment of his company, it was clear that most employees knew of this practice. This certainly doesn't promote trust and respect. In fact, it creates resentment.

Reflect on and examine your personal leadership model

Just as I had that *"Aha"* moment when I got bit by my own rattlesnake (a softer way of saying "I Got Fired"), each of us has to really take the time to examine just what kind of impression we are leaving behind as a leader. What do your footprints as a leader say about you? What will your leadership legacy be? What are your personal plans as a leader for next year and beyond? What are you doing to improve the impact you have on people? Who is responsible for your personal growth and success?

Self Analysis—look for your rattlesnakes

To be an effective leader, regular self analysis and reflection is absolutely critical to your personal growth. Start by asking yourself the following questions:

- What do you want people to say about your impact as a leader?
- What do you want people to say about you as a business person?
- What do you want people to say about you as an individual?
- What do you want your leadership legacy to be?
- What wisdom and intellectual knowledge will you implant in your employees?
- Are you a mentor?

No, we can't be absolutely positive about what people are going to say about us. But, if you have some form of a rattlesnake buried in your leadership model, kill it now. Even if you don't have a rattlesnake, take the time to really look at yourself in the mirror. To learn from your mistakes you have to first admit that you've made some. *I sure did*.

Outside Assessment

As successful executives, you deal with the urgencies of running a company on a **day-to-day** basis. You may consider having an outside firm do an assessment on your company. The very practices and characteristics that help you do this on a daily basis may actually be preventing you from seeing the 'big' picture with a fresh, open mind while subtly diminishing your diagnostic skills. Before you can solve these types of nagging problems, you must first accurately diagnose them. **It's easy knowing a problem exists, but much more difficult to put your finger on its precise cause and cure!**

An impartial **business assessment** offers a pair of "outsider" eyes with in-depth industry experience, which can help identify the most serious challenges you face.

Real value is built into the business assessment process through identification of challenges, along with recommended actions to specifically address the issues. It's all about knowing what your true critical constraints are and then focusing your efforts to solve them.

The assessment process conducted by the right professional firm is almost like going to your doctor for an annual physical. Generally, clients come to my firm, **CEO Strategist,** showing symptoms, but usually they aren't aware of the core problem or understand its cause. A **thorough, no-holds barred assessment from an outside perspective allows for total objectivity.**

One former CEO Strategist client (a $75 million electrical distributor) once described the process this way...

"It felt like taking a punch in the gut, but it will open your eyes to reality!"

It is equally important that the assessment is performed by someone who is honest, and not **necessarily nice.** This means they won't sugar-coat the issues. To be valid and offer true insight into your current situation, **business assessments should be conducted by someone who has "walked in your shoes"** someone with actual, hands-on experience and **not** by someone with only "academic" training or someone who has been groomed as a "consultant," but who never had to make payroll!

Lessons Learned

What are the take-aways from the **business assessment** process? Based on past experiences from assessments across many industries, you can expect to learn that:

- *Cherished beliefs are not always true*
- *Change is a function of future state minus current state, as well as a reflection of plan clarity and resistance*
- *The gap between 'world view' and 'world reality' will be more clearly defined*
- *Organization structure is a function of work*
- *People truly are your most precious business asset*
- *Success requires a platform created from the bottom up (not the top down!)*

Develop a complete and accurate picture.

What is really wrong? What is unique about your problems, if anything?

Attempts to resolve problems and get back to profitability often fail because we don't understand the problems in general. We don't get details specific enough to formulate solid resolutions achieving a complete and accurate picture of the situation **"The Real Deal."** This is absolutely essential so that everyone can see and understand collectively to allow collaboration aimed at restructuring for the Turn-A-Round or contingency planning process.

Understand the purpose to be served

You and your executive team must answer the question, what are we trying to accomplish? What is our purpose? You need to be data and goal specific. Becoming profitable is an unacceptable response. You must identify all contributing factors to your lack of success. Stating simply that "it's the economy" is not acceptable. Once you identify the other factors beyond that of the economy, then you must determine exactly what you should be doing and what your objectives are. You must develop a common understanding of and a universal commitment to the objectives. This commitment must come from not only your executive staff but from every employee within your organization. Failure to be data and goal specific often leads to disruption. You end up working on something that should have just been scrapped in the beginning. This creates wasted effort and doesn't produce results. You don't spend $6000 to fix a car that's only worth $2000 in tip top shape. Holding on to obsolete myths or beliefs only blocks progress.

Hanging on to old Joe who has been there fifteen years just because he's a nice guy is not acceptable if in fact he really retired five years ago and just shows up to collect his paycheck.

The "Real Deal" Criteria

The criteria are really a result of determining what "The Real Deal" is. Once you know that, you have a solid foundation on which to build the restructuring or contingency plan. What needs to be fixed, improved, corrected or avoided to achieve optimum results? Define the criteria for optimum resolution clearly as people often migrate to acceptable minimum actions and never ask what the ideal resolution should be. This is especially true if past performance and culture has been created under mushroom management tactics and lack of communication in a fearful autocratic environment. This destroys morale creating a rapid increase in employee turnover. The assessment process can help you define that criterion.

I learned a long time ago that "Profit is <u>NOT</u> a Dirty Word." In fact that is the title of my last book.

Well, Profit is also **"Not a God."** It is essential for survival of the organization but profit must take its place of importance behind the employees because they hold the power to create profit or lose it. They can also save it from many predators including the incompetence of upper management, dysfunctional family management, and apathetic foreign ownership.

Those who put profit ahead of their employees will create a culture within the workplace that breeds distrust and paranoia. Most employees devote a major portion of their lives to the job. Many "live to work" instead of "working to live." They need more from their job than just a paycheck. They deserve an environment that encourages initiative and empowers them to use that initiative. They need leadership that understands that listening to the employees is a prerequisite for success. Executive management has responsibility for the direction and results of the organization. The key role of the executive team is to establish and execute company strategy. The single most important determinant of long-term success, as mentioned before, is communication. Every employee must understand and support the strategy, especially during tough economic times.

Problems with staffing and retention may not be due to bad hires or a low unemployment rate. In fact, they may be related to *poor management insight* by not recognizing your employees as a core competency in your business strategy. Although employees may not fit the strictest definition of a core competency, it is a fact that your employees are the ones responsible for creating many of your core competencies. It is an **undisputable fact** that failure to recognize the importance of employee contributions will lead to failure regardless of your business strategy. Your contingency or restructuring plan cannot succeed without paying attention to this part of the business.

You must facilitate your employees' involvement and feedback into this process.

Even the brightest, strongest and most successful leaders within the industry are challenged during recessionary times. Even those of us with scar tissue, experience from past recessions, find that leadership becomes much more difficult in a declining economy. You may feel like you are just starting down the first big hill of a roller coaster ride. You may envision the next couple of years as high risk, high stakes – a time filled with uncertainty and ambiguity, but, we need to set those thoughts aside. Guard against creating a self-fulfilling prophecy of "doom and gloom." It is time to reach within, time to find whatever higher power you believe in, time to demonstrate the kind of leadership that can deal with these turbulent times.

Take a look at the following generic example of what you might expect from an assessment.

BUSINESS ASSESSMENT—GENERIC EXAMPLE

Note: This assessment is an accumulation of factors represented by several unidentified companies and should be viewed for example purposes only.

XYZ ENTERPRISES

OVERVIEW

This Assessment Review document is based on a detailed review of the information package provided by the Executive Management team and an on-site visit by CEO Strategist. Multiple group and private interviews with all senior managers and several key individual contributors were conducted by Dr. Rick Johnson. Findings in this document were reviewed in a late afternoon briefing with the ownership team.

It should be clearly stated that XYZ Enterprises has done many things right. The Company has an excellent reputation in the market place. They are well respected, have a good product line, an exceptional fill rate (96%), and the company is ISO certified. The executive staff recognized the forces of change and has taken steps to prepare the company for growth in the new millennium. It is easy, as an outsider, to only focus on negative issues, but the intent of this assessment is to bring to the forefront issues of concern that, in our estimation, need executive management attention.

XYZ Enterprises has been run in an exceptionally lean mode. In conjunction with below average profitability there has been a very limited investment in the proper infrastructure of the organization to stabilize the company and prepare it for the current economic decline. The following issues were noted in our assessment and are addressed in this report:

- Executive leadership
- Compensation
- Communication
- Strategic Planning
- Organizational Structure
- Culture
- Operational Management
- Systems Technology

SALES COMPENSATION PLAN

The Current Sales Compensation Plan is stated as a plan with a base salary plus an incentive. In reality, it is a total commission plan with an annual fluctuating base draw against commission, which is dependent upon annual territory gross profit dollars. Car expenses are rolled into this plan. Seven salesmen are currently exempt from this plan until their employment guarantees expire. This leaves fourteen outside sales personnel participating in the plan. There is no inside sales incentive plan, and, in fact, the inside sales personnel really function as customer service representatives. The basic problem with the current plan is that we believe it was written more as a method of managing the sales force instead of a means to reward those sales representatives who help achieve and support management objectives as well as increase in market share.

Incentive plans cannot, and do not, replace good management skills. Compensation should be based and measured on results and should avoid activity measurement, ownership and governance issues. The current organizational structure is not consistent with the planned growth anticipated by ownership. It is somewhat of a flat-line structure, which tends to encourage micro-management. This structure of management methodology will not support the strategic initiative of expansion and growth. The basic platform for a strategic plan emphasizing accelerated growth is a solid management team that empowers their employees and encourages them to use their own initiatives. However, you must have dedicated and committed employees that have taken ownership of the strategic initiatives. During our interview process, there was some indication of intimidation due to this hands-on micro-management style, as well as an acknowledged presence of perceived intimidation due to the employment of the owner's spouse. Regardless of the position, duties of title held by the spouse, she is still the owner's wife and the employees recognize and acknowledge that. Before you can structure the management framework to support the desired growth, you must complete a strategic plan that identifies all the resources necessary to accomplish that plan (this is discussed in more detail in the strategic planning section). The owners desperately want an answer to the question, *"How do we go forward and grow this business without destroying interpersonal relationships in the process?"* The potential conflict and animosity that this situation could create would effectively paralyze any strategic process. That would be a shame as XYZ Enterprise demonstrates huge potential in a growing market. This situation is one that will get worse as time progresses, as there is no clean exit point or closure to this ongoing discussion.

STRATEGIC PLANNING – COMMUNICATION

Although your current year business plan is of primary importance, it is also important that you create a vision of success and a feeling of hope within your entire company. Morale and turnover are major contributing factors to your current inability to maximize success. Employee confidence in company leadership and perhaps the company itself has faltered. It is imperative that you regain the confidence of your employees, rejuvenate their initiative and empower each and every one of them to contribute to XYZ's success. The entire Executive Staff must commit to the business with a passion. People must set high personal and departmental objectives and achieve them. Communication of the new direction, the new vision and the new mission is essential. This communication must be continuously repeated. Share information, show appreciation, celebrate your success and most importantly, *"listen to your employees"* and allow your staff to demonstrate leadership. The development of a strategic plan is an excellent vehicle that can be used to get employee buy-in, gain respect and prove that your testimony of empowerment is more than lip service. The real value of the plan is not in the finished product, but in the involvement of your employees in the development of the plan. In reviewing your strategic initiatives and the current budget it became apparent that it lacked a **"what if"** analysis. Additionally, the plan is not complete and has not been formalized. Although the concept of the plan addresses the basic issues of cost containment creating a breakeven at current revenue levels, it neglects to address the possibility of failure to meet budget expectations. A *contingency plan must be developed* addressing tactical maneuvers that result in black line budgets with stagnant growth and black line budgets with a 5-10% revenue decline. This pessimistic plan should be far-reaching and include reductions in executive staffing and branch consolidations. In fact, review of the decision not to close the Alaska branch may be prudent in next year's plan. Core competencies should be matched to customer expectations with the minimum amount of overhead required to maintain a lower revenue stream. Decide and keep only the necessary people and processes to survive. Based on the sessions with the Executive Staff, I have confidence that there is a high probability that you can achieve your established objectives. However, you must complete and formalize your current and next year plans recognizing critical constraints, identifying milestones and developing accountability with timely corrective action scenarios. Realize that your contingency plan is a survival plan and should not be entered into with a haphazard approach. Objectives should include:

- Margin improvement on all sales
- Overhead reduction in all departments
- Customer service must not decline
- Inventory reduction – receivables and cash flow analysis extremely important
- Trend line key ratios
- Restrict or eliminate overtime
- Investigate part time and temporary employees
- Re-investigate benefits for employee co-share
- Re-analyze all expenses – cell phones, laptops, T and E, janitorial and other service costs. Other non-revenue producing costs should be minimized

MARGIN EROSION AND STAGNANT GROWTH

Margin erosion is a common problem in the distribution business. The Margin enhancement programs we discussed should take control of this problem on your distribution side. However, it is more than optimistic to expect that you can impact margin more than a couple of points. Quite the contrary is true on the manufacturing side of your business. This is your **"diamond in the rough"** that has been abused and ignored for the past five years. Your margin on this business has been well below the industry norm since 2006 and you have lost over 8 points in margin the past two years. XYZ hasn't successfully instituted a price increase since 2004. You have stabilized your work force by bringing your pay scale up to market values to protect *"tribal knowledge"* but you have not passed the first penny of these cost increases on to your customer base. Additionally, your sales last year and year to date have decreased.

CURRENT YEAR STRATEGIC INITIATIVES – COST CONTAINMENT

In reviewing your current year initiatives and your cost reductions, I was pleased to see the structure, control and accountability demonstrated. Be careful not to over structure control by using project management on insignificant issues (if the bathroom needs painting, *just do it*). Structure and map only those issues that are revenue producing or cost containment issues. The fact that you have been able to show a small profit **at current revenue levels** should give your team and your financial institution confidence going into next year. As I discussed, your forecast and initiatives cannot stand on their merit alone. You must be able to drill down and demonstrate factually the "how" in accomplishing these objectives. This, in itself, will demonstrate credibility and instill confidence creating a reasonable success factor. You need to identify key indicators that your executive team can use to monitor and manage each initiative. As I mentioned, I was impressed with the structure and accountability you have built into your plan. Adding key indicators will help you track your progress more effectively.

E-COMMERCE – COMPUTER SKILLS

XYZ Enterprises has a nice website; however, it is strictly a "vanity site." If XYZ is going to reach its full potential and launch strategic initiatives to grow the business, then E-business must become an integral part of that plan. A transactional website needs to be developed. Analyzing the level of computer skills for the owners was like trying to play with a Christmas toy whose batteries were dead. This skill level must be enhanced to become part of the strategic initiatives. In our recommended actions we have included a "PC Boot Camp" to address this issue.

SYSTEMS AND TECHNOLOGY

The company utilizes a system that is three generations behind in technology. The largest issue is that there is no one within the organization with any real knowledge of what IT resources actually exist or how to use the toolset. The organization is limited by what other people tell them. This is potentially a very dangerous situation.

- The function is essentially leaderless, as the key skill sets/ knowledge must be in software, programming, and process design/implementation. No one with such skills exists in the company.
- Current software is woefully inadequate, and not having e-mail in a company that is projecting growth to $40 million is as effective as trying *to nail Jell-O to the wall with a sledgehammer*.
- To make maximum use of system technology, good process design skills must exist in the company. We see no such experience/skill at XYZ Enterprise.

The company has little or no idea of how to utilize e-business tools to improve sales, customer fulfillment and take cost out of the supply chain.

PURCHASING AND INVENTORY CONTROL

These issues also fall under the category of operational efficiencies. An inventory reduction program needs to be instituted, focusing on dead or aged inventory and vendor returns. A target turn rate of 6 or better needs to be established.

Local inventories need to be monitored and justified versus centralized inventory. Perhaps a Special Performance Incentive Program (SPIF) for purchasing could be instituted, focusing on the following objectives:

- $2,000,000 inventory reduction
- 50% reduction in aged inventory (12 months or older)
- Increased turn rate to 6.5
- Target vendor returns @ $500,000+
- Improve fill rate 25%

SALES MANAGEMENT SYSTEM AND STRUCTURE

Prior to implementation of a new sales compensation program and part of the readiness factor to the strategic planning process, development of core sales management and accountability objectives are critical. The sales organization needs to be redefined in support of the strategic initiatives developed to reach the revenue goal established by executive management.

- Establishing new sales model supportive of the strategic plan
- Process control and accountability measurement
- Pricing structure and strategy including segmented pricing
- Proactive focus specific targeted outcall programs
- Activity Based Sales Management
- Best practice sales audit

SUMMARY

It is obvious to CEO Strategist that the direction of the company is solely determined by **"reactionary"** response to circumstances and trends, which in themselves must have significant evidentiary history. The issues addressed in this assessment are critical to the future success of XYZ Enterprise. The quantity and the magnitude of the issues discussed suggest that the critical mass of the company alone has been sustenance to profitability in spite of the problems and challenges faced by the company, even though the level of profitability has been unsatisfactory. As we enter into the new millennium, time may be running out. In dealing with tough economic times, doing nothing is not an option. XYZ Enterprise must get up to speed and grow market share. They must avoid the downside risk associated with these problems that could leave them at a serious competitive disadvantage. Ultimately, that disadvantage could send XYZ into a **death spiral** forcing the unplanned sale of the company or crisis restructuring under a panic response management mode.

Avoiding the Death Spiral

||

Sometimes things just happen. Sometimes economic crisis can overcome our ability to cope. Maybe we lose focus and take our eyes off the ball. Maybe we don't recognize the signs. Sometimes it happens quickly due to a loss of a major customer or loss of a major product line. Sometimes it is a slow, gradual process. Market share seems to evaporate; gross margin exhibits an extended period of decline.

Morale suffers, employee turnover increases, net profit declines, costs seem to get out of control and losses become imminent. Some Owners, Presidents and CEO's who find themselves in a situation facing these warning signs may actually contribute to the creation of **"The Death Spiral"** if they aren't careful.

What is **"The Death Spiral"** and how do you know if your company is in one?

"The Death Spiral" can become fatal if not corrected immediately. This fatality can be brought on by many factors including economic turbulence. It can develop from the process of building an infrastructure ("Ivory Tower") prematurely based predominantly on the self-gratifying needs of our ego. It can also be created by the failure to deal appropriately with economic decline as mentioned in the opening of this chapter. Whatever the reason, the warning signs generally appear and, if ignored long enough, red ink from losses on the profit and loss statement will become the megaphone that finally gets your attention.

If it becomes an infrastructure problem that doesn't have a revenue stream of sufficient magnitude to support the fixed costs it generates, then the infrastructure must be torn down and rebuilt. Unfortunately, however, late recognition of the problem can cause the CEO or Owner to resort to a mental mode of retrenchment that could evolve into "Panic Response Management."

Panic Response Management is, in effect, crisis restructuring. There's nothing wrong with crisis restructuring by itself. However, this restructuring is more apt to occur from the bottom-up versus the top-down. In other words, revenue producing functions or people may be prematurely cut. These people or positions may be, at a minimum, covering their variable expense and contributing to some degree toward fixed costs. This creates a redistribution of fixed expenses which may now jeopardize the profitability of some other segment or division. This can create pressure to close other divisions and business segments or cut deeper into revenue producing functions that are contributing at least a portion to fixed costs, thus creating **"The Death Spiral."**

To most of you, this may sound ridiculous or even laughable, but it really does happen. The right approach is to view restructuring from the top-down, including taking a serious look at corporate and/or family overhead. You begin this diagnosis by asking questions like the following:

- How do you define your business strategy?
- How do you communicate your strategy to the employees?
- How would you define your company's competitive advantages?

- What are your strategic initiatives?
- What changes have had a significant impact on your business?
- What keeps you from being the most efficient and effective source for customers?
- What competitive advantages do your competitors have?
- What is the competency level of your executive staff?
- How do you rate yourself with respect to the success of the Corporation?
- What volume does the top 10% of your customers represent?
- How many of your customers represent 80% of your revenue?
- Do you measure account retention and growth?
- What is the turnover rate of your sales force?
- What is your overall corporate turnover in personnel?
- What percentage of your customers considers you to be their number one supplier?
- Have your average sales per invoice increased or decreased over the past three years?
- What single thing has had the greatest impact on your company's profitability?
- What single thing has contributed the most to your decline in profits?
- How does your company compare to the industry par report?
- What metrics or industry surveys are available to you from your trade association?
- Do you have a strategic plan?
- Do you have or promote a culture of cost containment?
- Do you provide functional leadership or do you dictate as a management style?

- Is there accountability within your executive staff and your upper management?
- Is there accountability within your sales force?

Get each member of your executive staff to go through this exercise for each department. When all the soul searching has been done, meet with your executive team to review the entire process and formulate a contingency plan. What is the situation you are really facing? If you are the owner or the CEO it is often difficult to admit the facts.

If that's the case, it is highly recommended that you hire an outside pair of eyes to help you through this assessment process as defined in the previous chapter. During the final assessment review you should be able to understand the scope and severity of the situation you find yourself in.

You **can** find a cure for "The Death Spiral." You **can** stop the spin. But, like convincing yourself to go to a doctor to get a professional diagnosis, you must start with a self-imposed reality check.

Step back; shut your eyes to the forest surrounding you and the swamp filled with alligators. Let your brain sort through the images created by your internal assessment. Deep down, the answers are there. You should now be able to clearly define and recognize the challenges you face. If the problem happens to lie within the executive staff and you own the company, don't languish in self-pity. Don't immerse yourself in the delusion that you're going to wake up tomorrow, look in the mirror, and see the **"Jack Welch"** of your industry staring back at you. Be smart enough to swallow your pride and ask for help.

The Assessment is Complete – Now What?

You have now completed an assessment on your business (see sample assessment in chapter I) and have figured out what the **"Real Deal"** is. It's now crunch time. You need to determine how to "Stop the Bleeding" under the economic turbulence that exists today. It's time to tear the Profit and Loss (P & L) statement apart to determine exactly how to become or maintain profitability. In an unprofitable Turn-A-Round situation you may find that pressure from the bank increases monthly. It's time to **"Stop the Bleeding"** and develop a satisfactory outcome. A satisfactory outcome requires the development of multiple budgets that can be presented to the bank in an effort to keep their continued support until you can make the business profitable. It is the foundation of contingency planning.

Contingency Planning

A "**Contingency Plan**" is a plan developed for a specific situation when things "could" go wrong or are going wrong. Contingency plans include specific strategies, initiatives and actions designed to deal with identified variances to assumptions. These variances usually result in a particular problem, emergency, or state of affairs. The plan also includes a monitoring process and "triggers" for initiating planned actions. They are required to help businesses recover from serious incidents or economic crisis in the minimum amount of time with minimum cost and disruption. Contingency planning is a management process that identifies potential impacts that threaten an organization and provides a framework for building resilience and the capability for an effective response and possible recovery if required. Once the initial contingency planning session is complete, ownership must decide exactly who will be part of the contingency planning team to execute the plan.

MULTIPLE BUDGETS

The platform for contingency planning due to a financial crisis is the **multiple budget process**. This contingency budgeting process is survival action planning and should not be taken lightly. It should not be entered into with a haphazard approach.

Objectives include:

- » Gross margin improvement
- » Increased market share
- » Decreased overhead
- » Cost containment – Death by a Thousand Cuts
- » Stable customer service
- » Supply chain management
- » Retrenchment – reduction in force if necessary

So Where Do We Start?

STEP #1

All budgets generally start with a sales forecast. Go back to the Vice President of Sales and request a new, realistic forecast. By the way, sales management is intimately involved in this process. Chances are the new realistic forecast received from the sales force is going to be highly optimistic. It is by nature difficult for any salesperson to forecast anything other than solid growth regardless of conditions. This is especially true if their incentive is based on revenue growth. The Chief Financial Officer (CFO) takes that forecast and using historical percentages creates a proforma (a projected Profit and Loss statement based on the forecast). Unless your sales force is unique and turned in a forecast showing no growth or a revenue decline, this forecast and proforma becomes a basis for your **"Optimistic Budget."**

STEP # 2

The next step is to take the current year's actual performance and extend it through year-end and determine the profitability or the extent of loss expected. Additionally, take the prior year's actual Profit and Loss statement and post it openly in the "War Room." I mention "War Room" because you must have a convenient, confidential place for your contingency planning team to meet regularly and develop your plan. It's called a "War Room" because there can be a lot of blood shed involved in a situation when the company faces substantial economic crisis.

Create a proforma for a realistic forecast and a catastrophic forecast just as you did for the optimistic forecast. These three proforma's become the platforms to build your three new budgets. If you are in the first half of the year, you use last year's actual numbers as a basis for determining your three new budgets. If you are in the latter half of the current year and can accurately predict year end results without the impact of any of the changes discussed in your assessment process then use that annualized proforma as your basis point.

The three budgets you need to prepare are called **"The Catastrophic Budget," "The Realistic Budget,"** and **"The Optimistic Budget."**

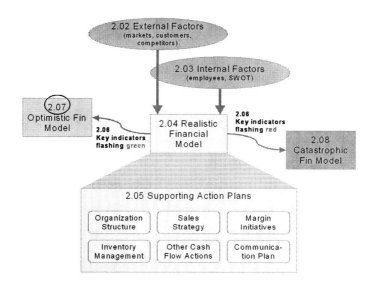

Caution: Don't Place Significant Relevance on the Numbers

USED. THESE NUMBERS ARE FOR EXAMPLE PURPOSES ONLY. FILL IN THE COLUMNS WITH YOUR OWN NUMBERS.

Optimistic – Budget Forecast

An optimistic budget is based on an expectation that economic decline will bottom out and market conditions will start improving.

Optimistic		Current Year	Next Year
Sales Revenue			$ 82,000,000
Gross Profit	22%		$ 18,000,000
Platform year Expense		$15,400,000	$ 15,400,000
Resulting Net profits/loss B4 Tax			$ 2,600,000
Break Even			
Desired profit	5% ROS		$ 4,110,000
Needed expense reduction/margin improvement			$ 1,510,000

Table I --- Optimistic Budget

THE OPTIMISTIC BUDGET CALCULATION

In calculating the necessary expense reduction and margin improvement the optimistic budget takes your platform year proforma revenue as the forecast. You could even adjust it by a small percentage according to individual circumstance. The idea is to demonstrate credibility in recognition of the possibility that conditions can become much better than anticipated. In that event, you are prepared to execute according to plan. Your budgeted revenue becomes a higher number utilizing historical data and percentages; you calculate your gross profit dollars. You then take your platform year's budgeted total expense (without any restructuring adjustment) and subtract that from the gross profit dollars. This shows your resulting pretax profit or loss.

Cost Reduction Needed ------------ $1,510,000.00

You have now calculated the net combination of expense

reduction and/or margin improvement necessary to achieve the objective of the optimistic budget. You must now focus on the realistic budget.

Realistic Budget Forecast

Your realistic budget can show the balance of the current year adjusted for current conditions to an expected level of sales of $77,000,000. This is considered realistic based on current backlogs and market conditions.

Realistic		Current Year	Next Year
Sales Revenue			$ 77,000,000
Gross Profit	20%		$ 15,400,000
Platform year Expense		$15,400,000	$ 15,400,000
Resulting Net profits/loss B4 Tax			—0—
Break Even			
Desired profit	2.5% ROS		$ 1,925,000
Needed expense reduction/margin improvement			$ 1,925,000

Table II --- Realistic Budget

THE REALISTIC BUDGET CALCULATION

In calculating your necessary expense reduction and margin improvement the realistic budget takes your platform year proforma revenue and decreases it 5 to 20%. This may vary according to individual circumstance. The idea is to demonstrate credibility in recognition of the possibility that conditions can become much worse than anticipated. In that event, you are prepared to execute according to plan. Your budgeted revenue becomes a lower number recognizing economic turbulence; next you calculate your gross profit dollars. You then take your platform year's budgeted total expense (without any restructuring adjustment) and subtract that from the gross profit dollars. This shows your resulting pretax loss or profit.

Your objective in making a presentation to your bank should

be to convince them that you will end the next year with an achievement somewhere between the realistic budget and the optimistic budget. If your presentation is done well, backed up by facts with definitive initiatives and action plans, the bank will probably believe that you will end the next year somewhere between the realistic budget and the *catastrophic budget*.

That's okay because that means you have stopped the bleeding and will end the year a stronger company, in control of your destiny and with the ability to turn next year into a very profitable year.

Cost Reduction Needed------------- $1,925,000

You have now calculated the net combination of expense reduction and/or margin improvement necessary to achieve the objective of the realistic budget. You must now focus on the catastrophic budget.

Catastrophic–Budget Forecast

You have now calculated the net combination of expense reduction and/or margin improvement necessary to achieve the objective of the optimistic and realistic budget. You must now focus on the catastrophic budget.

Catastrophic		Current Year	Next Year
Sales Revenue			$ 75,000,000
Gross Profit	19%		$ 14,250,000
Platform year Expense			$ 15,400,000
Resulting profits-Loss			($1,150,000)
Desired profit (Return On Sales)	0 R.O.S.		
Needed expense reduction/margin improvement			$1,150,000

Table III --- Catastrophic Budget

The catastrophic budget shows an arbitrary Return on Sales (ROS) of 0%. This equates to a profit contribution of $0. Owners may wish to review this figure on a quarterly basis.

Catastrophic forecasting is a contingency planning exercise. Doom and gloom thinking has no place in the planning sessions. However, the team should be aware that failure to meet objectives for the current year and market conditions predicted for next year could result in the execution of your catastrophic contingency plan.

THE CATASTROPHIC BUDGET CALCULATION

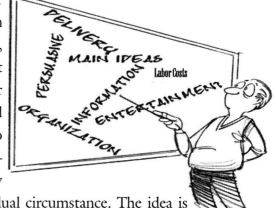

In calculating your necessary expense reduction and margin improvement, the catastrophic budget takes your platform year proforma revenue and reduces it according to your forecast. (a 20 – 50% decline) This may vary according to individual circumstance. The idea is to demonstrate credibility in recognition of the possibility that conditions can become worse than anticipated. In that event, you are prepared to minimize your losses by initiating your catastrophic budget. Your budgeted revenue becomes a reduced number from your platform year (based on economic predictions—this reduction could be substantial). Utilizing historical data and percentages, you calculate your gross profit dollars. You then take your platform year's budgeted total expense (without any restructuring adjustment) and subtract that from the gross profit dollars. This shows your resulting profit or most likely your resulting pretax loss.

Cost Reduction Needed ------- $ 1,150,000.00

There could be a slight reduction in variable expense due to reduction in sales, but for the purpose of this exercise it isn't significant enough to include in the calculations.

This exercise now tells you exactly how much cost reduction and/or margin improvement is required to reach break even.

Closing the Gap

The three budgets indicate exactly how much cost reduction will be necessary to meet specific profit objectives established for each budget. The catastrophic budget may actually acknowledge a forecasted loss or break-even at best. Now it's time to close the gap and create the actual contingency plan. This plan should list detailed strategic initiatives, action plans, critical constraints, milestones and key performance indicators to be used in the accountability process. All numbers and spreadsheets showing data crunching must back-up the contingency plan. The methods we previously mentioned that are used to "close the gap" are:

- Reduction in force
- Cost containment (death by a 1000 cuts)

Gross profit improvements may not be realistic due to the market dynamics during economic turbulence. Each budget should be categorized to reflect how the "Gap" (deficit) is to be closed.

Reduction in Force			
Line Item	Head count reduction	Department or Division	Total Net Savings
Optimistic	0		$0
Realistic	10		$350,000
Catastrophic	15		$400,000
Cost Containment		Death by 1000 Cuts	
Line item	Decrease from prior year		
	Realistic	Catastrophic	
Inbound Freight	$100,000	$100,000	
Interest	$300,000	$300,000	
Executive Pay-cut	$400,000	$400,000	
Profit Sharing	$100,000	$100,000	
Legal	$ 30,000	$ 30,000	
Security	$ 52,000	$ 52,000	
10% Tax	$ 20,000	$ 20,000	
Freight	$ 50,000	$ 50,000	
Dental	$ 28,000	$ 28,000	
Misc	$ 15,000	$ 15,000	
Overtime	$ 10,000	$ 10,000	
Variable Cost Reduction	$ 350,000	$ 350,000	
Additional Exec Pay Cut		$ 100,000	
	$ 1,460,000	$1,560,000	
Net change	$ 1,460,000	$1,560,000	
Summary of Gap Closures			
Expense Category		Realistic	Catastrophic
Reduction in force		$ 350,000	$400,000
Cost containment		$ 1,460,000	$1,560,000
Margin improvement		$ 0	$0
Totals		$1,810,000	$1,960,000

Table IV --- Closing the GAP

Summary Mini-Proformas	
Realistic	
Sales	$77,000,000
Gross Profit %	20%
Gross Profit $	$15,400,000
Expenses ($15.4m - $1.81 cost reduction))	$13,590,000
Profit	$1,810,000
R.O.S.	0
Catastrophic	
Sales	$75,000,000
Gross Profit %	19%
Gross Profit $	$14,250,000
Expenses ($15.4-1.96)	$13,440,000
Profit	$810,000
R.O.S.	0
OPTIMISTIC	
Sales	$82,000,000
Gross Profit	$18,000,000
Expenses ($15.4-1.46)	$13,940,000
Profit	$4,060,000

Table V --- Summary of MINI Proformas

Operational Strategy

RED LIGHT—YELLOW LIGHT—GREEN LIGHT

Once the budgets are compete and the GAP closures (cost reduction initiatives) are identified, you must determine the timeline for execution and at what stage of economic crisis the company is in. How do you know when to initiate further cost reductions, when to relax and when to be on guard? In turbulent economic times, you must be able to act and react quickly. You will be observing numerous indicators. Interpretation and understanding of these measurement tools is critical. These indicators may include among others:

INTERNAL

- Cash to cash cycle
- Operating profit
- DSO-accounts receivable
- Payables ageing-trend line
- Gross margin %
- Gross margin $
- Quote activity
- Backlog
- Book to ship ratios
- Head count
- Specific initiatives
- Budget analysis
- Book to quote ratios

EXTERNAL

- Interest rates
- Manufacturing backlog
- Purchasing managers index
- Business publication reports

- Government statistical web sites
- Association reports

The red light, yellow light, green light scenario establishes what mode you should be operating in based on the key indicators you have established.

Red Light   → Catastrophic Plan
Yellow Light   → Realistic Plan
Green Light   → Optimistic Plan

In a Turn-A-Round or contingency situation you automatically implement the realistic plan in a precautionary status. You are in the yellow light mode. You determine when and if you move to either the red or green mode by tracking your indicators.

Caution is the Word of the Day!

EXAMPLES OF KEY INDICATORS

Green Light		
INDICATOR	SITUATION	ACTION
Cash Flow	Positive Cash Flow	Manage to Plan
Operating Profit	Profit to Budget	Manage to Plan
Top Line Revenue	Positive Trend	Manage to Plan
External Factors	Positive Trend	Manage to Plan
Yellow Light		
INDICATOR	SITUATION	ACTION
Cash Flow	Trend Flat	Stretch Payment Cycles
Operating Profit	Meeting Plan	Increase Turns
Top Line Revenue	Trend Down	Review additional RIF
External Factors	Loss of Contract	Review Branch Closures
Red Light		
INDICATOR	SITUATION	ACTION
Cash Flow	Decreasing	Executive Pay Cuts
Operating Profit	Not Making Plan	Manager Pay Cuts
Top Line Revenue	Indicators Down	Planned Reduction in Force
External Indicators	Indicators Down	Crisis Cost Containment

TableVI --- Key Indicators

Preparation and Implementation

You now must prepare to present your multiple budgets and plan. If you are simply in a contingency situation your presentation is strictly internal to your employees. If you are in a Turn-A-Round restructuring situation you may have to make multiple different presentations to your bank and your vendors. However, before we get into execution of your contingency planning let's talk about how you view the situation you are faced with. Remember.....

Tough Economic Times could represent a "Window of Opportunity"

The state of the economy is a fact. How you feel about that fact and what it means to you personally is a belief. Your beliefs have a major impact on your employee's attitude. Beliefs that drive your sales behaviors are the keys to becoming successful in a down economy. If you believe that this economic crisis can provide you with opportunities, then your attitude will drive the behavior of your employees.

The Sales Person's Belief

One salesperson might believe that a "bad" economy means it's going to be harder to make a sale.

"It's just not possible to hit my numbers when the economy sucks."

Another salesperson might believe that a "bad" economy means you can now win lots more business.

"I am a good salesperson and I am prepared for this downturn. We have quality value propositions coupled with our ability to reach out – network and build customer relationships is far superior to the competition that generally only has price going for them. I know I can take business from the competition."

So, ask yourself these questions:

1. What Do Your Salespeople Believe?
2. What Do You Believe?
3. Is Your Glass ½ Full or ½ Empty

If you believe the glass is ½ Full, then you believe there is a window of opportunity built on the following foundation:

- Market share growth normally occurs in the down cycle
- High unemployment creates opportunities for the upgrade and recruitment of quality people from the competition
- Cost containment means trimming the fat from the "Top Down" – NOT the Bottom Up
- You take the "Smell the Blood" approach ---- Taking

advantage of vendor discounts and special promotions because inventory management has always been one of your core competencies and you are now in a position to capitalize on it.

- Refocus on customer service
- Refocus on best practice

If you believe the glass is ½ Empty, then you have adopted an attitude that may demonstrate fear, panic and confusion. Your leadership model becomes one of panic response management built on the following foundation:

- We must fight to keep from losing customers – cut prices
- We need to cut cost and the quickest way is a reduction in force (RIF)
- Cut expenses to the bone from the "Bottom Up"
- We must "Stop the Bleeding" which includes
  » RIF
  » Cut commissions
  » Sell off inventory
  » Reduce services

During economic turbulence, judgment can become cloudy and you can confuse personal needs with business needs. This means you put your personal wealth and objectives ahead of the business needs and objectives. This is a major mistake.

Attitude

This is Not the Time to Panic. Yes, there are economic problems, but there are also opportunities! Leadership during these tough economic times is about <u>not panicking</u>, and that's exactly the message I want to get across...don't panic! Panic causes knee jerk reactions, and they're rarely correct. This *Economic Panic that could be caused by "Media Sensationalism" can create* a knee jerk reaction that negates effective leadership.

Panic Creates Fear ----- and Fear

- Paralyzes Potential
- Ruins Relationships
- Sabotages Success
- Inhibits Initiative
- C i r c u m v e n t s Creativity
- Promotes Poor Productivity

I Fear Nothing!
I Fear Nobody!

Competition

We must understand the difference between panic and caution.

Panic – (noun) -- a sudden overwhelming fear, with or without cause that produces hysterical or irrational behavior that often spreads.

Caution – (noun) a prudent forethought to minimize risk: a warning, a precaution.

Deliberate leadership, clear thinking and solid strategies lead to success in any economy. *Panic leads to failure.* As leaders we need to be deliberate, thoughtful, and take the actions necessary to stabilize the future of our individual businesses.

The Pygmalion Effect

The wrong attitude can create a Self Fulfilling Prophecy. It's called the Pygmalion Effect. You must believe in yourself. You must believe in your own ability, the ability of your team. You must have the will to succeed even though times are tough. You must openly demonstrate the desire to succeed. Look inwardly at your own thoughts. Thoughts are powerful as they shape your attitude and your attitude shapes your beliefs which control your actions. Hard work is a direct expression of your beliefs. Effective leaders fall back on the five basic principles of success.

1. Commitment with a passion --- Leaders must demonstrate a commitment for success that leaves no doubt in the minds of their employees.
2. Realization that "you don't have to have all the answers." Seeking input from employees and openly discussing ideas and strategies is the best way to demonstrate a confidence in the team you have and the employees that will execute your vision.
3. Empowerment and Delegation
   Delegation is the handing of a task over to another person, usually a subordinate. It is the assignment of authority and responsibility to another person to carry out specific activities. Delegation, if properly done, is not abdication. The opposite of effective delegation is micromanagement, where a manager provides too much input, direction and review of 'delegated' work.

   Empowerment refers to increasing the spiritual, political, social or economic strength of individuals. It often involves the empowered developing confidence in their own capabilities. It allows a subordinate to make decisions, i.e. it is a shift of decision-making authority from one organizational level to a lower one. In the sphere of management and organizational theory, "empowerment" often refers loosely to processes for giving subordinates (or workers generally) greater discretion and resources: distributing control in order to better serve both customers and the interests of the company.
4. Employees are the most precious asset --- This means you

must walk the walk and invest in employee development and employee training even more during tough economic times. Employees are the profit and success creators of every organization.

5. Communicate intentionally and effectively following these ten tips.

- <u>"Manage by Walking Around"</u> – Get out and meet your people, talk to them, show an interest in them and in the job they are doing for you. This includes everyone from the forklift driver to your Vice President of sales. Everyone likes to know they are appreciated.

- <u>Eliminate unproductive</u> – unnecessary lengthy meetings. I know a CEO that refuses to allow chairs in the conference room. All meetings are held standing up. I don't believe there is a company that exists that can't do a better job making their meetings more productive.

- <u>Written communication</u> should be precise and clear. Don't write like you are a journalist for *USA Today*. Avoid excessive and lengthy diatribes that become confusing.

- <u>Create flexibility</u> in your organization structure. Rigid organization charts that are too restrictive can get in the way of getting the job done. Job functions and descriptions must have clarity but don't make them so restrictive and detailed that cross functional interaction, support and cooperation is limited.

- <u>Open your ears and your heart</u>. Learn to listen more effectively. That means becoming disciplined at not interrupting. You might be amazed at what employees will tell you if you just listen. You might be amazed at what employees can do for you and the company if you just let them.

- <u>Constructive feedback can be helpful.</u> Don't criticize the messenger. Frank opinions can be helpful if we allow our ego to get out of the way. There is no such thing as constructive criticism. Never criticize.

- <u>Put a filter between your brain and your lips.</u> A passing comment that seems frivolous to you could devastate your entire staff and you may never hear about it. Think before you react spontaneously. Don't say what you think they want to hear and remember; even the simplest or dumbest complaint to you is serious to the one expressing it. Be sensitive to the environment, the values and the culture of the person or persons you are communicating with.

- <u>Don't build a kingdom on the backs of your employees.</u> If economic times dictate cutbacks, layoffs and expense control. Start at the top. Share the pain. Look at corporate overhead, perks and fringe benefits of management and the executive staff. Consider a pay cut at the executive level.

- <u>Keep your hand on the pulse of your business environment.</u> Make sure you are well informed on the external and the internal environment of your business. Network with industry colleagues. Benchmark friendly competitors or businesses outside your region. Stay close to the communication channel of your vendors.

- ▪ <u>Make sure you have a definitive focus on employee training and development.</u> This must always carry a priority. Make sure your orientation program for new employees is continuously updated. The first sixty days is critical to retention.

Seek New Ways to Improve

If you are like most people, you are content with the status quo until something disturbs it. You should be constantly re-evaluating not just your sales plans, but all of your business strategies including policies, pricing, and employee performance. The idea is to eventually be as efficient and effective as possible so your company runs smoothly and profitably. Look closely at your competitors. Talk to business leaders you respect. Read business management books. Experiment; solicit feedback from your workers and customers. By doing several of these things you will accumulate a wealth of knowledge and experience crucial to the survival of your business.

Take Advantage of the "Window of Opportunity"

In a practical sense, what this means is that you view this time as providing you a unique *window of opportunity* to cut the non-profitable elements of your sales and marketing system away, to pare down to a dedicated and competent core, to sharpen the focus of every element of your system, and then to expand your market share so that you can weather the hard times and be stronger when the economy inevitably turns.

Evaluate your markets. Over the past few years have you stretched into markets which are not profitable? Are they unprofitably siphoning time and talent that could be more effectively focused on your core markets?

Evaluate your customers. The same approach applies here. You are probably losing money on a high percentage of your customers.

Get tough, prioritize and target your accounts based on the stability and likely growth of their business

Carefully and methodically examine each piece of your structure. Look at this temporary economic downturn as a window of

Is This My Window of Opportunity?

opportunity to jettison some of the policies and procedures that are vestiges of the past, and reconfigure your system for the next wave of future growth. Look at your inside sales department, customer service staff, marketing and sales administration, etc., with the point of view of reducing the unprofitable and focusing on the profitable.

Focus on gaining market share. Approach your good customers with sole source proposals. Capture the business and lock it up by forming long-term contractual relationships with those customers who are solid and supportive.

Finally, keep your antenna sensitive to the opportunities to add key salespeople, managers and executives. Many of your competitors will struggle to stay in business. Some good people will become available. The pool of available talent will swell. Look for opportunities to upgrade your personnel by picking off proven talent when it becomes available. Don't immediately hire the sales people your competitors have laid off. This may be the "Cream of the Crud." Do start recruiting the top sales people in your industry that may not have been interested in a career change in the past. They may have now changed their mind after seeing their friends being laid off.

Turn Your Vision into a Cause

"Leaders are visionaries with a poorly developed sense of fear and no concept of the odds against them." If you aren't a visionary ---- hire one ---- more importantly --- turn your Vision into a Cause.

I wonder how many of you remember the movie *Rebel Without a Cause*. This is a 1955 film directed by Nicholas Ray that tells the story of a rebellious teenager played by James Dean. In this movie James Dean played the part of a rebel but he had no cause that could provide direction, guidance or an ethic to get him on the straight and narrow path; the path to success.

Paradoxically to Dean in this movie, every effective leader I have ever known has had a vision. But, having a vision alone does not make you an effective leader. In fact there are hundreds of "Unsuccessful" companies and "Ineffective" leaders that have Vision

Our Future is Promising!

Statements posted on their websites, in their brochures and even posted in their lobbies - A Vision without a Cause?

You see, almost anyone can have a vision but if you have a "vision without a cause" you are just a dreamer. I have known plenty of dreamers in my lifetime whose ship never has and never will come in. One thing I know for sure --- ***If your ship misses the harbor --- it's generally NOT the harbor's fault.***

Let's Talk Profitability during Implementation

Simplistically, to generate a profit during tough economic times you must:

1. Increase gross profit
2. Reduce costs

You must be able to demonstrate credibility and believability in your business plan. Again, said in different terms to increase profit you must:

- Sell higher
- Buy lower
- Exercise cost containment --- RIF

We will address cost reduction first because it has the quickest return. Head count, a reduction in force, is the quickest way to take cost out of the organization. However, be aware of the **"Death Spiral"** mentioned earlier in this chapter. You must be extremely careful that you are not cutting revenue producing functions at the expense of gross margin, market share or service to your key customers or customers that are paying for that service. You may in fact lose some business from small customers. If these are the kind of customers that increase your service costs without paying for them, then that is a good thing.

Start at the Top

The first place to look, even before you analyze administrative support and warehousing functions, is the **"Ivory Tower."** In other words, look at the highly paid upper management structure. Perhaps jobs and functions can be consolidated. *Consider an executive pay cut that can be recouped as a bonus when the company becomes profitable again.*

Sales Force Reduction

Your revenue producers should be the last place to look when considering head count reduction. However, when faced with the situation of a reduction in force, view this as an opportunity to upgrade the sales force and eliminate any problems that you should have addressed months or years ago. Ask yourself this question about every one of your employees.

"If Sally or John Doe would hand in their resignation tomorrow, what would you do?"

The Answer

1. Don't Know (DK)
2. Pull out all stops to keep that individual because he or she is quantifiably one of your top producers -- -- a superstar.
3. Try to talk the individual out of resigning because he or she does a decent job and improves every quarter.
4. Shake the individual's hand courteously, say you're sorry to see that person leave and escort that person to the door with no remorse.
5. Wish him or her luck; escort him or her to the door and then scream Hallelujah because he or she is a problem that you have been avoiding dealing with for some time.

If you, combined with the input of your sales management, have more than a few Don't Knows (DK's), you haven't done your job well. If you have a lot of 4's and 5's this is the time to cut them loose. You may be able to do some territory consolidations and not lose revenue. At the very least you can upgrade and probably generate revenue growth. It is extremely important, other than your 4's and 5's that you do not cut the lifeblood of the organization by arbitrarily cutting revenue or gross margin producing salespeople as a cost reduction method. You may even want to replace some of the 4's and 5's as upgrades. That's not to say there should be absolutely no reduction in your sales force. I've yet to see an organization that couldn't do some trimming without impacting revenue and gross margin production. However, you must do it with the **careful precision of a surgeon.** Make sure you look at all the potential downside risk.

Once you make a decision, ***don't be afraid to pull the trigger.***

Basically, we're looking at three areas we must attack in a "Stop the Bleeding" situation to create profitability.

- Margin improvement
- Reduction in force
- Death by a thousand cuts – cost control

We already addressed reduction in force as having the most immediate impact on the bottom line. When doing a reduction in force, consolidations and branch closures must be considered and analyzed as to their contribution toward fixed costs. Of course there are other factors to consider depending upon your specific business, product line, customer base, etc. How will suppliers react to specific branch closures? Will consolidations jeopardize line retention?

Cost Containment --- Death by a Thousand Cuts

Death by a Thousand Cuts is nothing more than a detailed line by line analysis of the profit loss statement and the general ledger. Exactly what are the costs that make up each expense category? The following is a list of examples of cost beyond the obvious. These examples are not fictitious. They are actual examples from various companies that were facing restructuring.

- Consulting fees to a family member for services that didn't exist
- A 13 year old owner's daughter on the payroll for $25,000 per year to do a quarterly newsletter on her home computer
- The owner's housekeeper
- The owner's landscaper
- Leased vehicles for family members that are not employed at the company

- Large expenditures for jewelry and trips for the CEO's girlfriend
- Excessive conference expenditures that are really personal vacations
- Trips for friends and relatives not on the payroll
- Assets listed on the books that don't exist or are personal items located off the premises
- Rent or lease payments on condos or apartments in cities that have no justification from a business point of view; airplanes, charters, boats
- Excessive implementation costs for new systems
- Excessive bonuses
- Excessive executive salaries
- Excessive corporate overhead costs – glitz; things such as, expensive artwork, multiple club memberships, oriental carpeting and general expensive décor

Of course, if you are the owner of a privately held company you have the right to spend company money anyway you like within the parameters of the law. I'll qualify that statement by adding **"if you are profitable."** I add that "IF" because whether you are the owner or just "the man in charge" (CEO, President), you have an obligation to your employees. They depend on you to keep the company prosperous. Their livelihood depends on it. When looking at cost reductions in general, always trim the fat first. *Often times, owners and CEOs get so caught up in image and ego enhancement that trimming the fat alone is enough to get to break even.*

The next arena of interest when analyzing what it is going to take to "Stop the Bleeding" is taking a look at the assets. We're not talking about the assets that are essential to support the business. Again, we're talking about trimming the fat.

Areas to consider:

Real Estate

Do you have a lot of equity in real estate that can be sold to generate cash that you can replace at a much lower cost? Can you lease vs. own at the same or lower cost?

Vehicles

Does the owner need to drive a $100,000 Mercedes?

Other assets

Depending upon the type of business, there may be items that aren't necessary to the survival of the business; things such as, brand equity, trademarks, and product lines—territories.

Margin Improvement

With the competitive pressures of today's economic turbulence, margin improvement is your most challenging objective. As mentioned earlier the formula is easy.

1. Buy lower
2. Sell higher

However, it does get just a little more complex than that. The first area to attack is pricing. More often than not salespeople get in a rut when it comes to managing pricing. The attitude of "don't rock the boat," "don't fix it if it ain't broke," can often **generate huge profit leaks.** If you do matrix pricing, look at it carefully. Is it updated and reviewed often? Is it being applied correctly? Do your salespeople truly understand how to use it? Review all your contract pricing. Establish review procedures for contract pricing. Invariably you'll probably find a number of customers getting the advantage of contract pricing that doesn't fit the criteria that you had previously established. Implement service level pricing to recoup your cost of servicing the demands of smaller customers for non stock items, rush orders, order changes, restocking fees, conversions and other extras often supplied but seldom paid for.

Margin Impact

Margin management is not rocket science. Improving gross margin is simple. You must either raise prices or reduce cost of goods sold. But, there is a little more to it than that when you consider net profit. There may be a lot of hidden profits waiting for you to find them lurking within your pricing system itself. The good news is that this can produce tremendous gain with little pain. Go look at what you are doing and how you are doing it. Also, take advantage of opportunities on the buy side that are a result of the current economic conditions. I once had an owner tell me that during off hours when the office was closed, he increased his pricing matrix across the board 1 ½ percentage points without telling anyone. Nobody even noticed it for seven months and his margins improved dramatically.

Margin Implications

- Small changes in margin have large changes in the sales breakeven point.
- Sales Reps tend to get afraid of raising prices in soft markets. Some fear is real; most of it is chasing ghosts.
- They don't realize the consequences of failure, i.e. layoffs, lower service levels.

Activity Based Costing

Consider doing an activity based cost analysis on your entire account base. There is plenty of instruction manuals published on how to do this. I guarantee you that you will find some surprises. You should also consider implementing a "Margin Hold" system that forces management approval on orders entered below a minimum established threshold for gross margin percentage.

Buy Side Margin Improvement

The buy side of the equation also offers numerous opportunities for margin improvements. Approach all of your vendors. Don't be afraid to demand cost reductions. Your customers certainly aren't embarrassed to ask you. Review your entire purchasing organization. Do you have true buyers or are they simply order schedulers? Establish specific inventory reduction goals, turn-rate increase and fill rate improvement. Create an incentive based on the critical success factors on the buy side; factors such as, margin improvement, inventory reduction and inventory turn rates. Include any others specific to your initiatives for profitability. Remember, during tough economic times the magic words that will increase vendor discounts are "Big P.O." Try to take advantage of any **"itchy-scratchy"** opportunities (a new term I learned from some friends in Detroit). These are opportunities where you are buying a product from someone that uses the types of products you sell. The academic term is "reciprocity." The following is a checklist to review when considering margin improvement objectives.

- Do you have an established pricing policy?
- Do your pricing policies consider market segmentation, risk, service levels and value added?
- Is every customer buying off of the current price sheets?

- Are you charging freight out and other fees to the small accounts?
- Do all the inside and outside sales reps know that charging the last price paid is easy but wrong? It ignores small price increase opportunities.
- Is your counter sales/will call priced according to margin objectives?
- Do you have well trained buyers and do they negotiate?
- Is your purchasing/inventory control department managing the inventory well? Are they using the correct volume discount and item analysis?
- How do you measure your fill rate? Do you bench mark it to your competition?
- Do you have a system to review and evaluate your Return Goods Authorization (RGA's)?
- Do you charge for restocking?
- Are you getting the optimum discounts from your supplier and are you keeping the discounts as profit?
- Have you done a supplier profitability analysis?
- Are your customers profitable?
- Do you have significant supplier error?
- Do you have a vendor returns program and do you manage it well?
- Do you track your own and your suppliers on time delivery?
- Are you selling the right products to the right customers?
- Do you have an outcall program?
- Does your inside sales force understand the concept of up selling?
- Is your warehouse operating efficiently?
- Do you have a freight recovery program or do you fold under pressure and give it all away?

- Do you rank and evaluate your customers by gross margin dollars and gross margin percentages?
- Do you have an incentive program that is tied to gross margin growth both in dollars and percentages?

On the Sales Side

Ultimately to create margin improvement, your entire sales team must have good judgment of market potential as it relates to margin improvement. They must be self disciplined and make intelligent decisions based on fact. Each territory manager must develop his own plan for profit improvement and be flexible on the implementation of that plan. They must be action oriented and customer driven and yet be extremely conscious of profitability objectives.

Results must be measured against the plan. Trend lines need to be established both on revenue and profit growth. They must be able to see the rewards for their efforts. They must accept responsibility and accountability for improved profitability and achievement of established objectives. They need to understand activity based costing.

A formal sales plan is probably the most important activity that you should engage in during economic challenges. I am not talking about the typical Delusional Rectal Exaggerated Forecast (DREF) that many of us have become accustomed to. I am talking about a realistic, documented plan that lists the specific activities required to accomplish the objectives set for targeted accounts with identified growth potential. A sales plan is a schedule of events and responsibilities that details the actions to be taken in order to accomplish the goals and objectives necessary to be successful during these turbulent times. The plan ensures everyone knows what needs to get done, coordinates their efforts and keeps close track of progress. (Check out – "Turning Lone Wolves into Lead Wolves - 56 Ideas to Maximize Sales" – www.ceostrategist.com)

Sales plans must define the objectives, timeline and resources required to meet the growth objectives of the business unit, department, branch or specific territory. It should also detail how the company will achieve growth, profit and product objectives.

The market, like most markets, has not avoided transition. Contingency planning is an essential offensive strategy recognizing economic turbulence in creating competitive advantage. But, the overall business planning alone is not enough. Sales drive the company's success. Consequently, a sales plan must become mandatory if you are to succeed in this economic environment.

Analysis of opportunities is useless if it doesn't degenerate into work. Sales planning, by definition, results in action plans for individual territories outlining specific target accounts with defined goals and initiatives.

Territory Planning

The individual territory may find that its success in their own market depends upon the business segments they service and their willingness to compete within these segments. This segmentation is often defined by the buying habits and the individual needs of its members. A critical factor in developing the individual territory sales plan is understanding and differentiating activity based on market segmentation. Understanding local market segmentation starts with profiling your customer base. Demographics and customer's "Rules of Engagement" are typical criteria (chapter VII details sales planning as an offensive strategy).

Sales Effectiveness

It's really fun being a salesperson when the economy is booming. It is not difficult to do well and sometimes we can be lulled into a sense of eternal success that doesn't require a 100% effort. It can lead to a comfort zone that is not healthy for long term success. Make sure your sales force practices a sales effectiveness discipline that requires documented action planning for specific targeted accounts that support individual territory plans. Of course, these plans must be in alignment with strategic initiatives as well. Being realistic in our approach is even more important in turbulent times.

The "R" Word

Don't let that "R" word, Recession, introduce fear and uncertainty. Avoid those common mistakes salespeople make when times get tough; mistakes like, being slow to react, creating our own self fulfilling prophecy and becoming reactive instead of proactive in our approach. One of the problems with all of this talk about a tough economy is that once people believe times are really tough they start to feel negative about their business prospects and only tend to see what they believe rather than believing what they see. Once you believe that times are tough you tend to only notice articles, comments and statistics that support your beliefs.

The Sales Team

Let's Summarize

- The state of the economy is a fact.
- How you feel about that fact and what it means to you personally is a belief.
- *Your* Beliefs have a major impact on *your* employee's attitude.

Beliefs that drive your sales behaviors are the keys to becoming successful in a down economy.

What Do Your Salespeople Believe?

Reevaluate your territory plan, your sales management system and your sales effectiveness approach. I once told my sales force – "As *long as there are cars in the parking lot – they are buying something. It's your job to go out and get the biggest share of that business that you possibly can."*

Back to Implementing Your Plan………………..

The Bank Presentation

Your entire presentation to the bank must be positive. Do not dwell on the negatives of the past. You must acknowledge the past but don't beat a dead horse. You will actually cover the past in your presentation under the heading of **"What went right and what went wrong."** It is important that you schedule the meeting and you establish the ground rules.

- The Entire planning team and executive staff should be present
- The meeting should be held on your home turf
- Do not allow questions until the end of the presentation
- Create the presentation in summary format but have back up detailed slides available in case they are needed in the question and answer period
- Limit the presentation to 1 hour preferred if possible and absolutely no longer than 1½ hours plus the question and answer period

Presentation Format

Of course, there should be an introductory slide with the president, CEO or owner giving a brief overview and summary of the plan. Profiles on the executive staff, planning team members, should be reviewed to gain confidence in management competence.

The following topics should be briefly covered:

INTRODUCTION

- Basis for the budgets
- The basis should include an explanation of the factors considered, i.e. market share, inflation, margin trend and cost containment
- How the plan was developed
- How you are going to achieve the expected results
- What makes it credible
- What assumptions have been made

PRIOR YEAR REVIEW

- What went wrong
- What went right
- How things are going to be fixed-refer to later details—keep this general
- Extraordinary non reoccurring expense
- Success factors that carry over
- Negatives that carry over and how they will be addressed

NEW STRATEGIC INITIATIVES

- Identify specific revenue or margin enhancement initiatives
- Discuss key indicators
- Define milestones

SALES AND MARKETING

- Detail discussion on specific initiatives that relate to market share growth, margin improvement
- Discuss pricing control, review and initiatives
- Discuss forecast and how it was finalized with the object

being to gain creditability in the numbers

OPERATIONS

- Review initiatives
- Cost containment
- Process control
- Continuous improvement
- Key indicators

PURCHASING AND LOGISTICS

- Review initiatives
- Discuss inventory reduction and turn rates
- Vendor management and profitability
- Cost of goods reductions

HUMAN RESOURCE ISSUES

- Accountability
- Employee retention
- Up-grades
- Probationary programs
- Cost containment --- RIF

FINANCE

- Initiatives
- Ratio analysis
- Cash flow analysis
- Discuss the summary proformas for the Realistic and the Catastrophic budgets
- Refer to the forecasted P & L statements in the addendum for both the Realistic and the Catastrophic plans

Summation

To quote Wayne Gretzky the famous hockey player: Show them you are going to – *"Skate to where the puck is going to be."*

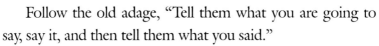

- Discuss the Red Light, Yellow Light, Green Light operational scenarios
- Review the highlights of the overall plan
- Close with confidence

Follow the old adage, "Tell them what you are going to say, say it, and then tell them what you said."

It is extremely important that the entire team displays unity and confidence in the plan as well as confidence in one another. Each manager in the organization should have some method of tracking his or her own departmental initiatives. Any method is acceptable from a computer program like "Performance Management" or "Project Mapping" to a simple spreadsheet analysis that lists the specific initiative, the expected result, which is responsible for accomplishing it and a time line for completion.

Once the bank accepts your plan and you have support, you must pull the trigger and implement the plan. This means you must restructure the organization. It is extremely important that the timing is precise. All actions must be done simultaneously, especially headcount reductions. Plant closures, job reassignments, branch consolidations and terminations all must happen in the smallest window of time that is possible.

It is imperative that you create one big giant shock wave that will immobilize the old culture instead of a lingering multitude of many that does nothing more than upset the entire company creating paranoia and distrust.

Get it done quickly, move on and be prepared to sell your plan to the rest of the company.

Presenting the Plan to Your Employees

The key to making a successful presentation to your employees regardless of the type of plan is integrity and honesty. Do not make promises you cannot keep. Do not sugar-coat the realities of the situation. Do, however, emphasize the positives of your plan whether it is a restructuring, contingency or even a Turn-A-Round plan.

It's Not all about numbers.

Your presentation to the employees must contain an overview of the financial challenges but you do not have to give the kind of detail that was included in your bank presentation. Your employee's main focus and main concern is their own personal security.

Any restructuring, benefit reductions, perk reductions or reduction in force should all come in one large action and not a series of mini actions. Get it done and put the pain behind you so you can honestly address the rest of your employees and tell them that their future is secure. If you can't be sure of that, then be honest about it.

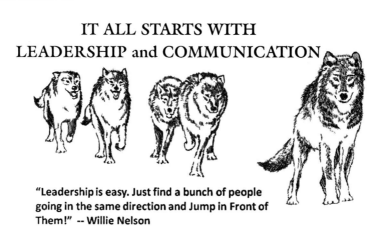

IT ALL STARTS WITH
LEADERSHIP and COMMUNICATION

"Leadership is easy. Just find a bunch of people going in the same direction and Jump in Front of Them!" -- Willie Nelson

Right! --- It's just not that easy Willie!

Communication and Leadership

Next to people, communication is the most critical element to success; whether you are in a growth mode, contingency mode, or you are facing a Turn-A-Round situation. However, in a Turn-A-Round situation or restructuring situation, failure to communicate has much greater consequences. Failure to communicate could ensure absolute failure. Communication is essential to developing trust. Trust is necessary to get people to reach down deep inside and give everything they have under the most difficult circumstances.

Colin Powell stated in an interview that as a young twenty-one year old lieutenant he was still trying to figure out the whole concept of mission and people when a crusty old Master Sergeant said to him:

"Let me make it clear for you, Lieutenant, so that you never ever doubt again what leadership is all about. Now, listen carefully. I ain't gonna repeat it. *A good leader is someone whose troops will follow him, if only out of curiosity.*"

I believe the reason people follow any leader, especially in the business world, is due to trust. The only way to develop trust is through communication. You have to talk to people with respect to gain their respect. You need their respect if you are going to develop their trust. You gain trust when people think you care as much about their welfare as you do your own. People have to think that you not only care about their problems but that you will make every effort to solve them. This is an especially difficult task in a Turn-A-Round situation where you have eliminated jobs. That is one of the reasons that it is critical to act quickly and swiftly when implementing your restructuring plan. *It is not only important to create a big enough shock wave to immobilize the old culture, but you have to convince the survivors that they are the keepers and you will all succeed together.* Leaders are respected for discipline. Survivors will recognize, if you gain their respect, that terminating people is part of the job; a sacrifice of part to protect the whole. Removing non-contributors and disruptions due to poor performance is in fact to their benefit.

WARNING---Do not under any circumstances keep an employee that is obviously a non-performer due to politics, tenure or relationship with the owner or anyone on the executive staff. This can countermand every honest effort and sincere communication made. It also sends a message of a lack of honesty.

Reduction in Force needs to be a "Surgical Strategy"

During tough economic times a reduction in force (RIF) often becomes a necessity as part of the contingency planning process. Let's face it, payroll expense is probably the biggest expense for the majority of companies in business today. Unfortunately, many leaders have a tendency to panic and make across the board cuts without regard for the long term effects, employee morale and the overall health of the company and its ability to weather the economic storm.

Gutless Management

Economic turbulence can create a window of opportunity to gain market share. At the very least it offers you the opportunity to fix and repair many issues that should have been addressed months or years ago but due to the fact that profit was easy to come by, many of these issues were ignored, overlooked or just swept under the rug. This is especially true if these issues had a direct impact on employee relationships. In other words, profit covers many sins. Some of those sins can be directly attributed to *gutless management*. I have to qualify that statement by stating unequivocally that I am a firm believer in servant style leadership. As leaders we need to serve our employees. However, servant style leadership does not mean that we accept incompetence, below average performance or comfort zone apathy.

I would doubt that there are many companies out there that don't have at least one or two employee issues that have been overlooked or ignored in the past for a myriad of reasons. *Let me tell you a secret*, the majority of your good employees know long before you do which employees are carrying their weight and are worth keeping. How many times have you struggled with an employee problem only to finally let them go and your employees said ---- "it's about time."

So, you are now faced with a necessary RIF due to economic crisis. It would be a big mistake to make arbitrary across the board cuts. Now is the time to make an across the board evaluation of every one of your employees. Start by looking at the functional contribution with respect to your revenue stream. Next look at the employee's contribution with respect to top line sales, profitability and their individual performance based on expectations; assuming you haven't set precedent with exceptionally low expectations.

The Surgical "Pruning Approach" Strategy

No garden can flourish if it is full of weeds. Now is the time to get rid of the weeds first. Compassion is a wonderful thing and is often referred to as strength. However, in turbulent economic times, too much compassion can be a life threatening weakness. Keeping "Old Joe" around simply because he has been with you for fifteen years isn't a good enough reason if "Old Joe" hasn't been cutting it for the past five years. Keeping Sally on the payroll because she is your wife's cousin even though she just figured out how to use the copy machine after five years will do irreparable harm to your organization during tough economic times.

A surgical pruning strategy only begins with the precision pruning of the workforce. To strengthen the company during tough economic times means you must invest in employee development and upgrades while you are surgically making precision cuts in the workforce. You may terminate three low performing or non performing employees and replace two of them with higher quality, higher performing candidates. Sales personnel offer an excellent example of the opportunity for workforce upgrades that position you to gain market share during tough economic times.

The surgical approach is simple. Recognize the necessity of trimming costs but at the same time recognize the opportunity to invest in upgrading your workforce and investing in customer development and employee training. Don't cut training. Now is the time to invest more into training as it can create or maintain competitive advantage.

Even a Surgical Staffing Strategy Requires a Plan

A reduction in force of any size is not pleasant regardless of the economic challenge being sensationalized by the media. You are messing with people's lives; families are involved. You have a moral obligation to make sure that your actions are honest, ethical and above board. Yes, some people may suffer but if you are in a position that requires the sacrifice of some to save the jobs and livelihood of many then you have little choice. However, your decisions must be based on some basic premises. The following tips can support your decision making process:

- Make sure employees have had fair and consistent performance reviews. Determine with factual examples which employees are your top performers and which employees are below average performers. Review and analyze contributions to success. This will support your surgical pruning strategy when it comes to a reduction in force.

- Don't cut back on skills training and management development. It's easy to cut training but in reality it should be the last thing you look at. That doesn't mean you can't be a little more cost conscious about it. But don't eliminate training in its entirety.

- Look at compensation. You may have to take some executive pay cuts but at the same time, consider a base pay increase for those employees rated as top performers that create a direct contribution to profitability. This may be especially true for your sales people.

- Communicate --- the worst thing you can do is keep employees in the dark. Over communicate. Be honest and open with employees. They are not stupid. Tell them the truth and update them often. If you don't communicate regularly, employees will make stuff up in their own minds and what they envision is generally much worse than reality.

RIF – How Big – How Many?

Before you begin surgically pruning the workforce, you should create a surgical team that can analyze current and future staffing requirements. This is a basic part of your contingency planning process. Contingency planning is essential to recovery from economic crisis. Your team should consider turnover rates to determine how many positions are likely to become vacant through attrition. Layoffs must be looked at with respect to permanency or short term horizons. Redeployment of personnel is a factor for consideration as well as cross training employees in other functional areas.

Of course when dealing with any employee issue your human resource department must make sure that you are not in violation of any existing State or Federal laws. If you don't have a Human Resource (HR) department, you should hire an HR consultant to support you during the process. Consider the following:

- Which jobs or functions will be eliminated entirely?
- What contractual recalls may be necessary based on any contractual obligations?
- What are the severance costs and consequences?
- Who will be involved in RIF's selection and what will be the parameters?
- Should there be a D-Day to announce the RIF all at once or should the RIF be done over a two to three month period? (Note: one swift move is preferred as having the least impact to overall employee morale. Staggered cuts leave the employees wondering – who's next).
- What about timing? Some states may have specific notification statutes for large RIF. The WARN (Worker Adjustment Retraining & Notification) act may apply.
- What about the market impact? Your competition may use it against you. Make sure your team develops a

communication strategy for both the internal and external environment.

- Will the company offer outplacement assistance?
- If you are shutting down a branch, who and how will you oversee the closing? Should you offer a stay bonus for selected employees until the division is closed?
- What about waivers and agreements not to sue if you are offering a severance package for select employee - Check with your attorney.

Employees want to take pride in their leaders. They are eager to give their trust, but you have to demonstrate the kind of character as a leader that deserves that trust. Don't let the employees down. Character is built around a true concern for the people within the organization. It is based on fairness and consistency.

RIF PLANNING CHECKLIST

√ Communicate the business reasons that make the RIF necessary. You need to be able to document the RIF necessity with economic data that demonstrates changes in the economy and the industry. This is a time to open with your financial statements.

√ Make sure you involve legal council in planning the layoff. Consider obtaining waivers and releases in which employees agree not to sue in exchange for severance benefits where appropriate.

√ Clearly define the RIF plan other changes that will support the plan.

√ Outline in detail the process for implementing the layoff.

√ Be consistent in your actions and don't make promises you can't keep.

√ Clearly define the RIF goals to ensure that the financial

    objectives are in alignment with the contingency planning goals for the financial stability of the company.

- √ Evaluate employees' skills, job performance and personal contributions to determine which employees will be included in the RIF. Be fair and consistent.
- √ Kill all the "Sacred Cows."
- √ Provide severance benefits where appropriate to minimize individual consequences.

Gaining Credibility

Leadership and communication are intertwined. They go together. **Leadership without communication is like a gun without a bullet.** It may look impressive, but it can't do anything. Leadership and communication help create solidarity. Solidarity implies a unity within a group that enables it to manifest its strength and exert its influence as a group. Unity implies oneness, especially of what is varied or diverse in its direction or clarity. This is particularly true when a business is struggling for survival. Unity describes the inner relationships of individual parts making up the whole. It is an achievement that demands the probability of action and leadership. That action, that leadership, if appropriate and precise, leads to trust.

The very first step required after a restructuring or contingency process is mass communication. It is virtually impossible, as President, CEO or COO to get out in the field and talk to every employee face to face; although that should be a priority during the course of the year. An acceptable alternative to reach every employee is teleconferencing or Gotomeeting.com. A second alternative is the production of a video tape presentation to every employee simultaneously. Mandatory viewing of every employee at a pre-selected time is essential. The video or teleconference should send a positive message addressing the following issues:

- Reasons behind restructuring
- Future objectives
- Commitment to success
- Discussion of survivors and honesty of future actions
- Motivational teamwork discussion
- Framework for future communications
- Discussion of trust and values
- Answering questions posed by employees (at least 30 pre-selected questions and others asked by panel of employees)

It is necessary to solicit ahead of time questions to be asked by employees. These questions are the heart of what's now on the employee's mind. Do not duck the tough ones. The employees will know and you will lose respect, trust and credibility. Face the issues head on with honesty. Supervisors can generate these questions from the employees' company wide and submit them for review. Every question does not have to be addressed, but the most relevant to the employees must not be ignored. The answers need to be rehearsed ahead of time. The President facilitates this Q and A session but can direct different members of his executive staff to provide the answers.

A handpicked group of line employees should be selected to ask these questions of the executive staff on tape or as part of the teleconference. This is only the first step. Answers must be open, honest, sincere and complete. This is the very first opportunity since the restructuring announcement to demonstrate leadership, respect and trust.

Communication will hold the company together. It is especially important that the message is consistent throughout the management team. As important is the demonstration of respect, trust and leadership. However, no one factor plays a more precious role in building and preserving that trust amongst the employees, than communication. **It is a make or break issue.**

It is not only important that the President knows what the CFO and the COO are doing but he must also know what they *intend to do under every circumstance*. Once those determinations are made, the employees deserve to know what is planned if they are expected to execute with precision. People need a keen sense of trust and a feeling of being part of the plan. The communication network should connect all employees. Everyone needs to be a part of the overall plan. Miscommunication, rumors and garbled messages cause conflict and distrust. Don't settle for second rate communication, it's too critical to success. If you avoid informing all your employees, specifically on matters that affect their lives, you are playing with fire. **This kind of action breeds resentment, mistrust and paranoia.**

"Be aware that the single greatest problem with communication is the illusion that it has been achieved." (UNKNOWN)

We all communicate daily. We practice communicating daily, yet experience confirms that most often we fail to communicate effectively. Add to that obstacle the fact that you are undergoing a restructuring process and the challenge of communicating effectively seems overwhelming.

Why do we have problems communicating?

- We are always in a hurry
- We do not listen well
- We are afraid to ask questions
- We don't seek feedback or provide it
- We use unclear words or symbols
- We do not have the trust and respect of the person we are

Listening skills are especially important. Proof that you are listening is in your actions. Don't ask someone if they understand. Ask them what they are going to do.

All He Does is Talk – Talk – Talk

communicating with
- We fail to anticipate
- We think people can read our minds
- We think people have the same perspective as us

Difficulty in communication is enhanced when you are involved in crisis situations or adversity of some nature. Contingency planning or restructuring due to economic crisis certainly qualifies under those guidelines.

Listening is a Key Communication Skill

Listening should dominate your interaction with your employees. Distractions need to be removed. Trust must be developed. You must have a sincere desire to understand. You must be aware of individual needs. Be attentive and don't assume anything. Ask for explanations. Don't interrupt because you want to talk. Try to keep an open mind. Be compassionate and don't react too quickly. Avoid talking about yourself. *These are the basic rules of communication*. Remember: You and the person you are communicating with are trying to create a shared meaning.

Meaning is not in the words or symbols you speak. Meaning is in your head. The symbols represent your thoughts. Your goal is to get your meaning that's in your head into their head, and hopefully, you will create a shared meaning. If you are not being understood, then you are probably not using very good symbols/words to represent your thoughts. Try again until he/she understands your meaning. Communication is shared a responsibility. In order to have effective communication, both parties must have the desire to communicate. If your employee has a problem, has a concern, or has a question, you need to give them the respect; listen and make eye contact. Ask questions. Avoid distractions. Ask them if you are interpreting their concern accurately. Don't make a decision right then. Take notes and analyze the situation at a later time. Suspend judgment. Both you and your employee need to help each other communicate effectively. Make sure they understand you and you understand them.

Leading is not a "Cake Walk" in Tough Economic Times

Determine who the real players are. You need to understand what you can really ask of employees during these times. Be careful of misplaced or misdirected loyalty. Be careful of false loyalty. There are limits. You need maximum loyalty from your employees during tough economic times. Make sure you know whom you can trust. Besides loyalty an equally important is the need for a high commitment to the job. Your team must have a willingness to hang tough. Commitment demonstrated by the leader can lead to commitment by the employee. Commitment is self-nourishing and it gives meaning to work. Employees will look to you first to measure your level of commitment. They want to take your pulse. They want to believe in you. They need a leader they can follow. It's imperative that you show no signs of weakness and you don't let them down. This goes for the entire executive staff.

Employee commitment will soar if you and your executive staff demonstrate a passion for success. Excitement breeds excitement. Success breeds success, the more consuming your desire to fix things, the more you demonstrate leadership and draw support from your employees. You, as President and your executive staff set the stage. If your company fails, chances are you did not set the proper environment for success. Your primary objective is to; **Create an attitude, Structure an environment and Develop your team.** Your intensity, your focus, your drive and your dedication along with these same attributes from your executive staff are the determinants of the level of commitment you get from your employees. Commitment won't survive if leadership doesn't exist. You must be proactive and publicly demonstrate leadership, confidence and commitment.

It is important to deliver a message of renewed life to your employees. Come up with an acronym that reflects the new strategy; "A new Vehicle for Success;" "The New XYZ Company Way;" anything that can be referred to over and over again to communicate progress and success. Speaking of success, it is also important to demonstrate success in some format early on. This is vital even if it is a small success or a new account. A reduction in Freight expenses, anything that can be attributed to employee contributions.

A Common Fallacy—Have All the Answers

A mistake many leaders make during contingency planning or the restructuring process is the self imposed responsibility to have all the answers. This is just not true. It is okay to admit to not having all the answers. Good leaders are willing to show their imperfections. Surround yourself with a solid executive team and you don't need all the answers. No one expects perfection, just leadership. Being *President doesn't grant you supreme knowledge.*

Are You Doing the Moon Walk --- Going Backwards While Moving Forward?

The death of Michael Jackson was a tragic event. No matter what you thought of Michael personally, there is no doubt that he was one of the most talented entertainers of all time. His singing and dancing talent was showcased so effectively by his performance in the video and album "Thriller." It will be remembered forever as the Capstone of his career. I, like millions of his fans, mourn his passing.

However, the one thing that I remember the most is his invention of the "Moon Walk." The "Moon Walk" is a dance move that looks as if you are going forward when in reality you are moving backward. Michael made that move famous. His tragic sorrowful death reminded me of that move. The Moon Walk itself brings to mind how many businesses often struggle to achieve success; doing things that are supposed to gain market share and create success. And yet, many find that even though they believe they are doing all the things the "experts" say they should be doing, real success eludes them. They feel like they are moving forward but in reality they are moving backward. They are doing the "Moon Walk." This can be particularly evident during tough economic times.

Make Sure you are Relevant and Current

You need to be relevant and current – don't get stuck in the past with past practice that may have put you in a comfort zone because business was so good the "fish were jumping in the boat." Most of the time there is no shortcut to success. Relevance is more than just following best practice. It is more than just developing a contingency plan. Every effective leader I have ever known understood this principle. They are aware that their impact on the success of their organization was based on their vision, values and core beliefs they shared with all their employees.

Focusing on "the positives of the past" is a valiant intention to be sure; I wonder, though, how realistic and relevant past practice is if past success was simply the result of economic conditions and not effective leadership with a solid management team. If that is the case, you will simply begin doing the "Moon Walk" with no real vision based plan to deal with the current economic situation. Good anecdotes, memos to employees and resting on past success and past practice with little success substance will not solve today's problems.

Being current and understanding the real challenges you face is just as important as making sure it is relevant. Running a responsible business isn't something you just decided to do overnight. Hopefully you have been making conscious best practice business decisions for a long time and you are still learning as you go. Every step along this path during economic crisis is important, from high-level market driven decisions to individual employee relationships. Take the time to review best practices as they apply to your business. Look at your processes, your procedures and your policies. Do they reflect good management principles or do they become a little spongy due to past practices? Are they relevant to what is happening in your markets today?

A Vision is still critical

Businesses focused on developing sustainable long term market share growth during tough economic times often have a longer time-horizon and a broader set of goals than companies that have not stayed current and relevant to their market place. Typically they are dissatisfied with the status quo and not only have developed contingency plans for the short term to deal with economic crisis but they have not abandoned their long term strategic vision for the company; albeit, they may adjust it according to current relevancy.

To succeed in today's economic environment, leadership must build a foundation that allows the creative energy released by employees to actually work. We must leverage employee dedication and sacrifice that stems from ownership of the Vision-Values and Core Beliefs that has been engrained into the culture of the organization. The CEO or owner of this type of company generally conveys a well-articulated set of principles that guide the business and help to instill the same values in employees. By declaring their goals publicly this type of leader inspires trust and respect which is the baseline for employee commitment to success during tough economic times and long term growth.

This broader vision of success requires new business tools, practices and relationships. Being receptive to new ideas and suggestions opens the door to an array of business opportunities. That's what being current and relevant is all about. You cannot afford to wallow in a pool of pessimism and past practice without opening your mind to new ideas and new options.

Be Open Minded

The internet revolution brought on many changes to the market place and presented enormous opportunity. Before this revolution took place, undertaking large projects, entering new markets or working globally was the exclusive privilege of large corporations and conglomerates. In this century, innovative use of 'virtual' corporations, strategic alliances and other partnerships and ventures means smaller companies can now compete and generate business outside their traditional markets. Communication technology allows global orientation for even the smallest business and the greater efficiencies that can be offered by a team of small players, enable these firms to perform on the global stage.

Dealing with economic crisis requires the application of sustainable business principles that are current and relevant. You must maintain a forward momentum regardless of circumstance. Realize that every problem and challenge you face on a day to day basis as a result of the faltering economy are the same issues and challenges faced by your competitors. Ask yourself this question, "Can you outperform the competition?"

Improvements in your sustainable business practices must come from new ways of thinking about meeting customer needs, and redesigning operations with a priority focus on servicing your customer. You can't afford to do the "Moon Walk" if you are to thrive during tough economic times. Prepare yourself and your management team to be forward thinking and open to new ideas.

Focusing on Qualitative Market Share Growth

One of the biggest challenges in creating a sustainable future and gaining market share in a tough economy is the ability to refocus policy and practices across a variety of functions. The focus on revenue growth was appropriate prior to the current economic environment when "fish were jumping in the boat." Today, however, focus must be on market share as opposed to top line growth. Remember, if sales decline by ten percent but the market itself declines by twenty percent, effectively you have gained market share. This is an important principle that everyone on your team must understand. High-performing organizations integrate market share focus and performance management best practices more than other organizations. Conversely, low-performing organizations consistently underutilize these best practices and lose focus on market share.

Execute the Plan

The inability of organizations to effectively execute their contingency or strategic plans is one of the major factors limiting success; success measured by market share growth. Recent management research and literature has thoroughly documented the importance of execution in creating success during tough economic times. Organizations execute their strategies through the creation of contingency plans and strategic initiatives, comprising any number of initiatives, programs and projects that become the vehicles for realizing the corporate vision that is current and relevant.

Whether a company ultimately succeeds or fails during these economic times depends on the effectiveness of the actions taken to deal with current challenges. Before these actions can be taken, however, companies must recognize these challenges for what they are to take appropriate actions.

The "X" Factor of Leadership

The "X" Factor

Some people believe there is no such thing as a "Born Leader." When people talk about born leaders, what they are really referencing is the "X" factor of leadership. What is the "X" factor? Simply stated the "X" factor is the willingness, the desire and the willpower to become an effective leader.

Effective leaders go through a never-ending development process that includes education, self study, training, experience and coaching and mentoring from one or several individuals that have a very positive influence on their personal development. Leadership is the ability to influence, inspire and motivate others to accomplish specific objectives. It includes creating a culture that helps direct the organization in such a way that it makes it cohesive and coherent keeping short term tactical goals and objectives in alignment with long term strategic initiatives. The success of leadership in this process is directly influenced by the individual leaders' beliefs, values, ethics, character, knowledge and skills.

Position and title may give you power but power in itself does not make you an effective leader. To become an effective leader there are specific skill sets that you must understand and master. This does not come naturally. It takes dedication, passion and commitment to the process. That commitment, dedication and passion includes a tireless effort to improve on specific skills and the development of a personal leadership methodology. This is often referred to as your personal leadership model.

If someone were to ask your subordinates to evaluate your leadership abilities, their response to this question would likely **not** be related to your character, integrity and values. Of course these are important to your success as a leader but people evaluate your leadership skills based on what you do to figure out who you really are. They are looking for that "X" factor. The "X" factor is what really determines if you are honest, ethical, fair, trustworthy and not self-serving. If the "X" factor does not exist, employees are likely to *obey rather than follow* and only do exactly what they are told to do and nothing more. If the "X" factor does not exist, your success in developing the skills necessary to become an effective leader is likely to be minimal.

The "X" factor shapes what and who you are as a leader. It involves everything you do and it affects the well being of the organization. Employees want to follow a leader they respect, one that gives them a clear sense of direction and a strong vision of the future. Ask yourself these questions to determine if you or other managers in your organization have the "X" factor.

1. How well do you know yourself with regard to self improvement and development?
2. Do you understand, admit and work on personal weaknesses?
3. Do you seek responsibility and take responsibility for your actions striving to reach new heights?
4. When things go wrong do you take the blame instead of looking for others to blame?
5. Does problem solving, decision making and planning come natural to you?
6. Are you a good role model and do you seek out employees with high potential to coach and mentor?
7. Do you truly believe in the value of your employees sincerely caring about their well being without being so compassionate that it clouds your judgment on competence?

So you believe you and your executive team all have the "X" factor.

As effective leaders you must be able to interact with employees, peers, seniors and many other individuals both inside and outside the organization. You must gain the support of many people if you are going to meet or exceed established objectives. This means that you must develop or possess a unique understanding of people. The "X" factor is the driving force that will help you develop these skills. Human nature is the common qualities of all human beings. People behave according to certain principles of human nature. Understand these principles that govern our behavior and success is imminent. Start with the basics by revisiting your college study of Maslow's Hierarchy of Needs. Armed with a refresher of this basic knowledge of human behavior you can now begin to reshape your personal leadership model. This is your manner and approach to providing direction, implementing plans and motivating people. If you have that "X" factor you can become a very effective leader. Effective leaders go through a never-ending development process. We never stop learning and we never stop growing. Keep working on your leadership model and share your knowledge and success with other potential future stars that have the "X" factor.

Now is the time - Get on the "Leadership" Bus!

The Nucleus

IV

CREATE AN ATTITUDE— STRUCTURE AN ENVIRONMENT—DEVELOP A TEAM

Close your eyes; let your brain sort through the images from the time you started the restructuring or contingency process, to your end game vision, five to seven years down the road. Be comfortable with your decisions. They were well thought out, necessary to rejuvenate the corporation. Don't languish in self-pity or doubt. Now is not the time to have second thoughts. Now it's the time to charge forward. You must take advantage of the immobilization of the old culture. You now have to create a culture shift. You must create an attitude, an attitude that promotes success.

You have named your plan "*The New (Your Company Name) WAY.*" Your restructuring or contingency plan may even be described as a small downsizing. Down play the consequences. The past is the past. Look to the future. Be sure that you were careful and precise in your communication and explanation to the employees. You must be sure that you are not wrapped up in the wrong grand illusion that everything is okay even if it isn't. The executive staff must deal with any sign of discontent, rumors or distrust immediately. You must maintain credibility. Talk to the employees, answer every question. Do not forget about the law of consequences. You reap what you sow. You must be cognizant of unintended consequences. As truthful as you try to be, employees may interpret hidden agendas. Make sure there are none. **Be honest and address the doubt**.

A decision creates proactive movement of some type. It either reinforces a current belief or projects a new and different direction and response. Now is the time to be careful with every decision. Anticipate each intended consequence as well as every possible unintended consequence. The very first step in structuring the type of environment for success is contingent upon creating the proper attitude in the work force. Don't be fooled by an illusion of wisdom on the part of the executive team. Cover your bet, feel the pulse of your employees with interaction and clear every issue that needs to be dealt with.

"SET UP A THIRD PARTY HOT LINE TO ANSWER ALL EMPLOYEE CONCERNS CONFIDENTIALLY."

Start the human due diligence process. Human due diligence answers the question "Do we have, and can we retain the psychological capacity to successfully create a winning and cooperative attitude amongst our employees?" Conducted properly, this assessment, this touching the pulse of your employees will identify the assets and liabilities that exist within the people organization. You must capitalize on the assets and deal swiftly with the liabilities. Hopefully, if you did your job right during the initial contingency planning process the liabilities will be minimal.

Creating an attitude means getting your employees to work with you. Accomplish that and the road to recovery is much smoother. Change can only be realized by our actions and our actions are controlled by how we think and feel. This composes our attitude. Consequently we must focus our efforts toward success with the right kind of attitude, an attitude of confidence and conviction. If your employees only work for you, they will tend to do only what is asked of them. Sometimes only enough to stay under the radar screen. They will demonstrate no initiative and take no risk. You can't afford that.

Release the Discretionary Energy in Your Employees

What is discretionary energy? Discretionary energy is the energy an employee uses when going above and beyond the call of duty to complete a task or get the job done. Every employee has discretionary energy. The amount of energy released and employed at work depends on their attitude, how well they enjoy being at work, how they are treated and how they feel about the company.

Discretionary energy can be the difference between doing what is expected and performing in an outstanding manner. Consequently, our people skills and leadership skills play a paramount role in determining whether employees give freely of their discretionary energy. Does that mean that we must let the inmates run the asylum and do whatever they want to make them happy; of course not. But, it does mean that we must utilize effective leadership skills in dealing with issues, problems and day to day training, coaching and mentoring.

Structure an Environment

Creating the right attitude is paramount to structuring the proper environment. Getting your employees to work with you and join in the search for better ideas, new methodology and higher profitability will transform your company from passive individualists to intelligent action takers and change agents.

You need **"Risk Takers."** You need **"Mavericks."** Identify every employee in that category and empower him or her to go out and get the job done. So what if they bend the rules sometimes. As long as they don't break the law, violate corporate core values or embarrass the company, *"Turn Them Loose."* You have everything to gain and nothing to lose. The employees will see this as a demonstration of trust and empowerment. Word will travel fast. Promote that concept. Send a monthly memo to everyone praising individuality that result in improvements. Title your memo, **"OFF the CUFF"** for it's informal straight talking honest feedback from the top. Reward and recognize the risk takers. Commend the change agents. Then align both management and the employees behind the new vision. Help them drive **"The New** (Your Company Name) **Way."** Support this new environment by sharing the vision, departmental goals and strategic initiatives. Publish the minutes to every executive meeting that is held. Hold nothing back short of personal issues. Be proud and announce the fact that there will no longer be secrets held under close cover behind the doors of the executive staff.

Educate

Educate your managers and supervisors for their new role in this new environment. Do not tolerate deception or deviation from attitude or your new structure. Teach them to be coaches, mentors and transmitters of directions. Educate line employees to make them know they are part of the plan, part of the new way. Teach them new skills for self-management, planning, team building, goal setting, risk taking, conflict resolution and negotiating. Show them you care. That's all part of structuring an environment.

The "New Way" is the new corporate vision. It's a mental picture of what the company is all about; where you want to go and how you are going to get there. This is the vision for the company. It does not reflect the personal idiosyncrasy of the CEO. It has a broad base of support and buy-in from the employees.

Empowerment --- Don't Micro Manage

I deal with a lot of leaders that confuse delegation with empowerment. I am often told, "I don't micro manage, I empower my employees." However, when we start digging into specific situations, we often uncover the difference between delegation and empowerment. It is really not that difficult to ascertain the difference. Delegation is simply getting someone else to perform a specific task for you.

"Tom, can you move these pallets for me to make some room for a new shipment coming in tomorrow?"

Empowerment sets a little higher expectation that encourages the employee to use their own creativity and innovation.

"Tom, our warehouse is getting pretty full and we have a new shipment coming in. Can you figure a way to solve this problem for me?"

In other words, just telling an employee what to do is not empowerment because it doesn't allow him to use his own creativity. In fact, many times delegation can be construed as micro managing simply because the employee feels offended that he is given directions that are too specific. So, if you even have the slightest thought that your employees may consider you a micro manager, try these tips and see if your empowerment skills improve.

- Analyze your leadership model. Do you hold things close

to the vest? Are you reluctant to share information? Are you afraid of giving up control? If you answered yes to any of these questions you have a challenge on your hands. Your answers may be very telling with regard to your skills as a leader. Remember, a leader is only as good as the people they surround themselves with.

Micro Management Destroys Trust

The easiest way to suppress discretionary energy, the energy given willingly – no matter what it takes, is a style of micro management that scrutinizes every decision an employee makes. It can kill their spirit. It destroys trust. If any of your employees even joke about you being a micro manager - back off. Where there is smoke there is usually fire. Micro managing may make you feel in control but in reality you are only hurting yourself and the company. It only limits an employee's ability to be innovative and creative. This can cost the company thousands of dollars because it is the creativity and innovation of your employees that maximize the profitability of your company.

Micro Management is a Symptom

Micro Management is often just a symptom of ineffective planning, too much compassion and the inability to judge performance and develop bench strength. Developing a strategic plan for your company is a very effective way to address any or all of these challenges. I often tell my clients that the most valuable part of a strategic plan is the development process itself. Running a company with a shoot from the hip mentality often encourages micro management and does not allow employees to develop their skills and maximize their potential. One of the many warning signs is a high turnover rate. The reason is simple; good employees just won't tolerate micro management and they will leave to find employment that will challenge them and help them grow.

Ten Tips to Avoid Micro Management

1. Try to understand your lack of empowerment-delegating skills. If you keep things too close to the vest because you fear losing control, you may need personal coaching to help you understand that empowerment and delegation will actually increase your control as it provides you with more time to plan and work on strategic issues.

2. If you lack trust in your employees remember the statement --- "Employees won't start trusting you until you start trusting them." If you absolutely cannot let go; ask yourself why you hired the employee. In the end if you can't trust them you need to replace them. If you find you can't trust any of your employees then you need help in developing your leadership skills.

3. Create a skills assessment inventory for every key employee. Supplement that exercise by creating a training and development matrix to improve the overall competency of the organization. Include yourself in the assessment. Communicate the purpose in a positive fashion to the employees.

4. Consider doing a 360 review that includes you as a leader or create an anonymous survey for employees to rate the entire management team, including you, and the company culture itself.

5. Utilize your skills assessment to make sure you have the right people in the right seats and identify future potential leadership.

6. Stop answering questions and start asking them. When an employee asks you what they should do, ask them what they think they should do.

7. Search for projects, issues or challenges that you would normally tackle and create a project team or empower an individual to solve the problem. Do this even if you think you have the answer.

8. Let your employees fail. The hardest thing to do is to watch an employee make a mistake. But, unless the mistake is life threatening or is going to cost the company thousands of dollars, it is a better learning process if the employee learns from his own mistake.

9. Provide more than just skill training and product training. Create an employee development program for those employees that show potential for future stardom. This development program must be based on empowering these employees to make tough decisions. Intern programs are also effective as a platform for development.

10. Results happen in various ways. Remember, you may have a specific way of doing things but it may not be the only way. As long as the employee is getting the results expected, give them praise. Your way may not be the best or only way.

It's About Leadership

Simply put, effective leaders don't micro manage. In fact, they cringe at the thought of it. Why? Because they recognize that one of their primary responsibilities is the development of future leaders for the organization. You just can't develop future leaders by micro managing.

Micro managing can be an indication of the following:

- Lack of trust in your employees. This is not good because it often leads to a lack of trust in you as a leader.
- Fear of lost control. This is often demonstrated by a parochial attitude about turf or position in the organization. This may also indicate a lack of self confidence and low self esteem.
- Panic response to emergency and crisis. The micro manager often feels alone on an island and when a crisis hits they may panic and respond reactively without much thought, planning or discussion.

Don't be afraid of the word "micro-management." Discuss it with your managers, your employees, and do an honest management self assessment. Trust your people to act and you may be surprised at their initiative, their creativity and their intellect. It may even seem like magic. Empowerment provides the freedom to act and it demonstrates trust and belief in the ability of your employees.

Consistency and Fairness

To create the proper attitude and structure an environment conducive to survival, growth and success, you must treat employees the way you would want to be treated. You must be a proponent of openness. You must be sensitive to their needs. You must understand the initial shock and the healing that must take place in the organization as a result of contingency planning/restructuring.

A cosmic truth states that you must give before you receive. Mandating new rules, stipulations, threats and unreasonable demands does not promote unity or trust. It is destructive to the kind of attitude required to succeed. Employee consideration and input is absolutely essential to structuring a new environment. You need employee support, trust and respect. But, you must give before you get. As a leader, you must know when to lead and when to listen before acting. Empowering employees allows them to use their own initiative, their own creativity and figure out things you'd never imagine they could accomplish.

Avoid Resentment and Rebellion

Change is tough in itself. Add the fact that a restructuring change or implementing a contingency plan is even more threatening and creates an enormous amount of resentment and fear. It is scary and disruptive, often times leading to rebellion. That is why it is so important to communicate well and build the proper attitude within your core group of employees. Structuring an environment that breeds success and promotes openness, honesty and trust is an essential ingredient to successfully executing your plan.

Keep Things Simple

Try to keep initiatives simplistic, realistic and achievable. Phase the initiatives so that early successes will come and be recognized. Complexity has no place. If the employees don't understand, no amount of effort will allow them to reach the desired results. Learn to listen to the employees. Nothing is more frustrating to an employee than a supervisor who will not listen to a solution to a problem that is so obvious the supervisor should have acted long ago. Structuring the right environment is not that difficult if you make your employees a priority.

Employees Need Recognition

Congratulations on a Job Well Done!

Every employee wants to feel that they have a voice and can be heard. They want to know that management knows they exist and what their contribution is. They want the satisfaction of doing a good job. They want to prove their talent to achieve the desired results. If they are challenged they will become self-motivated.

Employees Need Association with Others

People enjoy other people. They derive satisfaction from interaction with their peers. Recognition is icing on the cake. Employees find the social aspect of the work place rewarding if the environment is positive and conducive to success. Make coming to work enjoyable for your employees. Create ways to challenge as well as entertain the employees. Provide the opportunity for social interaction. There are a number of ways to do this from a once a week company sponsored lunch to monthly breakfast sessions with the president to talk about current issues and new events.

The "FUN" Relationship to Success

Having fun is the very first recommendation I give to anyone that asks me how to create success within their organization. I have always said that if you don't enjoy doing what you are doing, if you don't have fun doing it, then you should do something else because you simply can't excel at anything unless you really enjoy doing it. That means having fun. You can walk into almost any company and observe the employees for a short period of time and I guarantee you that the employees that seem to be having fun, those that display a real fondness for what they are doing are the ones whose performance will exceed expectations.

Those that have the frowns, those that are grumpy and those that are apathetic to what they are doing will not perform up to expectations. People that are too serious or take themselves too seriously rarely come up with new ideas. It is already proven by research that humor aids the healing process. I suggest to you that having fun and enjoying what you do is a key component to maximizing your success. I believe creativity and innovation are often spurred by having fun and doing what you enjoy doing. It's common sense. If you don't enjoy what you are doing why would you spend the time or energy to come up with new ways to do it or new ideas? Remember, new ideas are often just the coming together of several old ideas. However, if you are not enjoying what you are doing you won't even be thinking about old ideas let alone the combination of several.

Realize that it is quite a challenge to maintain a fun culture during a restructuring, implementation of a contingency plan or a Turn-A-Round. However, it can be done, but it requires a demonstration of respect and trust for the employee as the platform for structuring this type of environment.

Employees Seek Self-Esteem

Recognition and praise raises self-esteem. Positive feedback and ample communication allow employees gratification and a newfound confidence in the organization. To be successful, individuals must not only believe in their leaders but they must believe in themselves. Effective leaders promote a self confidence on the part of their employees that builds self esteem; the grass root for maximizing potential.

Employees Need to Feel a Sense of Power - Autonomy

Most employees derive satisfaction by having an influence over something or someone. A few leadership traits are inborn to some degree in every human being, some more than others. Allow the employees the opportunity to demonstrate leadership in some form or fashion. Create work teams, committees and projects that motivate by presenting the opportunity to make decisions and be a part of the overall process of turning the company around. Empowerment is the key to autonomy. Allow the employees to take risks and demonstrate initiative. The rewards are far greater than the risk. Give them some independence in choosing their work schedules or other factors that won't affect overall objectives. Be flexible.

Employees Seek Security, Fairness and Equitable Treatment

A common mistake some executives make is demonstrating insensitivity by making a big expenditure for some asset right after restructuring and terminating a number of employees. Don't do this. Go without no matter what. It is by far the worst message you can send. A personal experience I witnessed involved a president of a corporation that had just restructured, terminating 87 employees. He then remodeled the executive conference room spending over $50,000 which included a wall mounted big screen TV and remote control curtains. Obviously that disrupted any attempt at creating the proper attitude, not to mention the environment of distrust and animosity it created. You must make your employees part of your life. Acknowledge their presence, their contributions and praise them at every opportunity. But, be sincere. Jack Welch had a favorite method of sending personal handwritten notes to employees that demonstrated some form of success. Sincerity is a must. Handing out praise indiscriminately is not better than any praise at all. If you deliver praise the wrong way or for the wrong reason at the wrong time it can do a lot of harm. You must be specific about what you praise and why you are doing it. Do not make a big deal out of the ordinary just to hit your praise quota. If you praise employees for just achieving their normal expected performance it becomes meaningless and will not motivate. Additionally, when they do something outstanding, your praise means very little. Lastly, don't think that telling an employee that he has done a good job on twelve different occasions is a substitute for some other type or reward. Specifically a monetary reward and recognition of some type is essential for the outstanding performer even in tough times including a "Turn-A Round" or contingency situation.

Motivation

The employee issue cannot be emphasized enough. Tough times weigh heavy on employees. They know when a company is not performing without seeing the profit and loss statement. The good ones start to abandon ship and seek employment elsewhere. Add

Does He Look Like a Motivator?

restructuring and employee terminations to the formula and keeping your good employees becomes the most life threatening issue you are likely to face during tough economic times. Losing good employees has a high cost associated with it.

Ten Tips on Motivation

1. **Find the right job for the right person** - When people enjoy and are challenged by their work they become self-motivated.
2. **Empower and delegate** - Trust employees to make their own decisions and make their own mistakes.
3. **Co-operation vs. Competition** - Excessive competition destroys morale. When teams work towards a shared goal they become more motivated.
4. **Performance vs. "Presenteeism"** - Do long hours necessarily equal quality work? Look at whether your organization encourages a presentee culture rather than valuing performance and results.
5. **Involve employees in company development** - Keep employees informed on new developments in the organization and how their work impacts the company.
6. **The 5:1 rule** - Praise and recognize employees' successes five times as much as you provide constructive feedback.
7. **Job security** - Possibly the greatest single factor for a motivated workforce. How can you improve job security and fringe benefits?
8. **Lead your staff** - Enable managers to coach their teams and

create opportunities for people who are keen to learn skills and grow within the organization.

9. **Create a comfortable working environment** - Including relaxing the dress code where appropriate, developing areas for socializing, creative thinking, reading and giving employees quality spaces to work in (larger desks, quiet, natural lighting etc.)

10. **Treat employees fairly** - When people feel they are treated fairly they remain loyal to the company and motivated by their work. Perceived inequality of treatment leads to resentment, low morale and lack of self-motivation.

Frederick Reichheld's book, <u>The Loyal Effect,</u> points out:

"If you are losing employees, you are losing customers. On average, American companies lose half of their employees every four years and half of their customers in five years. This suggests that employee attrition may have a significant impact on customer loyalty."

I suggest that going through a restructuring or Turn-A-Round only accelerates that process. Ensuring that your employees continue to grow is an important part of the environmental process. Training is a key ingredient.

Revolutionary Change

Implementing contingency plans that incorporate restructuring borders on mastering revolutionary change. It requires facing the challenge of creatively destroying and remaking the organization to improve profitability. In order to succeed, the plan must be driven by leaders that inspire employee buy in, commitment, and support. They must have fresh ideas and the spirit and guts to make things happen. They must create a way of life by taking a risk and believing in the employees that have chosen to remain on the team.

Develop Your Team

Success of your Turn-A-Round or contingency plan not only depends on your employees but they are heavily reliant on the executive team and management structure you put together to lead the effort. This effort will demand a variety of different skills from your team leaders. You must be sure to articulate the plan clearly enough that it is understood by all and is strategically sound. Your executive management team must be aligned in support in their hearts as well as their minds. You have to make sure that this team not only demonstrates their competence in practical skills but more importantly they must demonstrate **a superior competence in people skills.** The attributes, values, personal beliefs and competencies are all important in carrying out the plan. You must put aside politics, ownership prejudices, personal feelings and biases. You must determine what the plan in its execution will demand from your leaders. If there is no doubt as to loyalty, commitment, tenacity and staying power then the time to act is now.

Remember, you must address any family issues that have a negative impact on meeting newly established objectives.

Replace any executive and upper management personnel that don't meet the minimum requirements necessary to see it through; including family. Assessment of your current management staff is mandatory. Listen to your employees. They probably can tell you more about the leadership of the company inadvertently than direct one on one interviews with the staff. Once you have chosen your team, you have just begun. You must create a mentorship within your own executive staff. Development of the leadership of your staff is an ongoing process. Personal action plans must accompany the Turn-A-Round plan. You personally by way of example must participate in all learning activities so that the process is taken seriously. No one is above improvement. Everyone can learn.

Winning organizations continuously build leaders at every level in their organization. Leaders who actively attempt to mentor and build other leaders gain respect throughout the organization and transfer knowledge, ideas, values and attitude about success. Your executive team must have the following attributes. They must:

- Demonstrate a sense of urgency
- Project and articulate the vision
- Create stretch goals
- Develop trust and a spirit of teamwork
- Develop realistic expectations for success
- Promote an environment of success, trust and belief

Your executive team must have an edge. They must be courageous enough to take risk and have an unrelenting readiness to act. Popularity is not a requirement but the ability to generate respect from the employees is without a doubt one of the most critical attributes. They must be relentless in their efforts, unconscious about personal sacrifice of their time and the willingness to go beyond normal expectations. Tough decisions are commonplace; uncharted territories will be the norm. Honesty and impeccable character is a must. Being decisive, doing the right thing, setting clear objectives, motivating and inspiring employees and creating a sense of urgency are challenges that must be met by all members of

the management team. Every single member of your management team has to make a difference. It's the price to play the game. It's part of the rules. Don't pay, don't play, it's as simple as that. You are not in a position to be overly patient with team members that can't **"Bump Bellies and Grunt"** to get things done in such a way that they command the respect of your employees.

There is a Difference between a Leader and a Manager

Make no mistake, to maximize your own effectiveness you have to be able to function both as a leader and as a manager. The trick is to know precisely when to go into the manager mode and when to become that servant type leader. This is true for your entire executive team. I once read a quote by *Vassilis Siakos* on the difference between a manager and a leader that stated:

"A Manager 'does the thing right' and a Leader 'does the right thing'."

That is quite a simplification. First of all, a manager doesn't always do all things right and conversely leaders don't always do the right thing. Oh sure, most leaders do the right thing most of the time, but what the "right thing" is can cause quite a debate and who gets to decide what the right thing really is? And who decides who and what is actually right?

Doing the Right Thing

Doing the right thing doesn't sound very complex for a person of character and integrity but think about this for a second. During my ten years as a Turn-A-Round specialists there were several occasions when I had to sacrifice the jobs of many to save a company and the jobs of others. Was that the right thing to do in the eyes of those that lost their job, their income, their security? If you were the wife, the husband or the child of one of those employees that were sacrificed for the sake of survival of the company would you think that it was "the right" thing to do? We are not talking about malcontents, under performers and employees with issues. We're talking about pure innocent sacrifice here. You too will have to face this kind of a decision while implementing a contingency plan or restructuring.

All of a sudden, "the right thing" gets a little more complicated.

Leaders Inspire Others to Greatness

True leaders inspire others to greatness. In spite of what may seem the contrary, being a true leader in times of sacrifice and turbulence is even more important than in normal times. However, it's equally important to adapt to the role of manager as well when sacrifice is necessary. I often talk about compassion as both a strength and a weakness when it comes to individual leadership models. I have met numerous CEOs that boast of long tenure employees. However, there are some that earn that tenure simply due to the compassion of ownership. Certainly compassion for people is a strength but it can become a weakness if it stands in the way of accountability and maximizing the effectiveness of the organization.

Do I look Confused?

There is a fine line between leadership and management; a line that is often shifting according to circumstance.

The Balance of Compassion and Performance

So how does an effective leader balance compassion with performance and accountability? A leader must demonstrate the need for maximizing performance to the team. This is communicated more by action than words. Tolerance for the lack of excellence or subpar performance sends a distinct message; the wrong message.

A leader must lead by example whereas a manager uses direction and enforcement of policy and procedure to accomplish specific tasks. Of course, a manager must also be able to lead as well.

Sound confusing? It is......... There is a fine line between leadership and management; a line that is often shifting according to circumstance. If you are going to maximize growth and profitability in your organization, every manager must become an effective leader. A leader encourages, leads by example, cares about the team and gives regular feedback. People need to be recognized and praised. A leader influences and inspires others to believe in themselves and to follow a vision for the future. Effective communication can stir emotions and emotions can become a powerful motivator. Communication is essential, but knowing when to go into the manager mode and become less a servant is also necessary. This mode should be the exception but it does exist for even the greatest leaders and it is necessary at times. In fact, the true test of an effective leader is that they know when to go into the manager mode.

Confidence, Self Esteem or Ego

We all have egos but effective leaders control their own egos and understand how to utilize their understanding of people to inspire peak performance. This is especially critical during tough economic times. Effective leaders are confident and have high self esteem without demonstrating arrogance. Leadership cannot be ego driven. Effective leaders are not only compassionate, but they are passionate about success and they make every effort to coach and mentor their team. However, a leader can't afford to waste too much time in the minutiae of the team. In fact a functioning team will solve many of its own problems and they are expected to. This happens when the right people are on the team.

Leaders lead by example, they delegate and empower people. They also seem to have a keen sense about selecting and developing the right people. That in itself is a key difference in transcending from being just a manager to becoming an effective leader. Selecting the right people with potential to excel and then developing those people through the coaching and mentoring process to achieve greatness is a primary responsibility of leadership. Effective leaders know precisely when to coach, when to mentor and when to manage.

Check Your Ego at the Door

A leader's role is to serve those people that report to him. He or she is not a dictator or a CZAR --- their ultimate role is to serve, to allow their employees to achieve their goals. It's a style that starts by asking: What do you want to accomplish, rather than telling them what you want them to accomplish? Effective leaders demonstrate a respect for employees recognizing their value as their most precious asset and the innovative use of planning and control systems demonstrates a unique ability to balance predictability with simplicity.

Don't be Arrogant—Follow these tips:

- If you start to believe you are special and nobody is as good as you, just look at the number of people in your industry, in your state, in your country. Then ask yourself; how many of this grand total of people even knows your name? Unless you're Tom Cruise or Angelina Jolie, chances are not many people really even know who you are let alone actually care how good you think you are.

- Arrogance is often just a mask that hides your personal self doubt. Try to figure out what is causing your insecurity and work on improving that area. But first you have to be honest with yourself.

- Speak clearly about other people in a positive sense. Make a special effort to ask questions concerning other people's activities and lives. Take the "I" out of your vocabulary and only answer specific questions about yourself but keep your answer short, brief and to the point.
- Make it a point to listen at least twice as much as you talk.
- Model yourself after the most respected people in your industry. Note, I said respected not the most successful. Success does not necessarily mean respect. It depends on how success is achieved and how success is defined.

Create a leadership survey and ask your peers and subordinates to actually rate your performance. E-mail rick@ceostrategist.com if you would like a template.

You are the only person that can affect a change in your thinking or your attitude. Your thoughts are powerful. They are energy. How you feel and how you act depends on your thoughts. Master your thoughts and **you** control your attitude.

So what's the difference?

How do you create a leadership model you can be proud of, one that speaks volumes about who you are and not what you accomplished? The answer begins by taking an inventory of your personal values. Your core beliefs and how you treat other people will speak volumes about who you are. It also reflects the size of your ego.

In reality if you are going to be responsible for the actions and results of others it just isn't good enough to be only a manager. Effectively, managing is about leadership. Personally, I believe to be really effective, there is no difference. An effective leader must be a good manager and a good manager effectively must be a good leader. The results will speak for themselves in the long run.

Reinforce the Real Purpose—Vision for Success

Remind your executive team continuously of the real purpose. Encourage them to form an alliance with your employees. You are all in this together. You must evolve into a cross-functional management effort with employee networks, clusters, adhoc task forces and the ability to accept and encourage mavericks that aren't afraid to "take calculated risks." Practice the power of appreciation, understand priorities and communicate them. Create religion in generating and sustaining the trust of your employees. Absolutely, do not let the old culture stand in the way of your plan. After all, that is the past. Your current plan is the future. Make sure your entire executive team is ready to accept the depth of commitment required to rebuild the organization. It requires patience, tenacity, understanding, competence, reflection and a willingness to recognize one's own weaknesses in an effort to negate those weaknesses with support from other team members.

A willingness to go the extra mile to reach and exceed the success levels necessary to create "The New (Your Company Name) Way." An abstract requirement during this process is the ability to imagine an end game vision that is plausible; a real purpose; the future you intend to create. You need to understand your boundaries and limitations from all aspects not just your financial limitations. Recognize that even though you believe in the executive team you have selected as agents of change, initially during phase

A Willingness to go the "Extra Mile"!

one of restructuring; they may be branded as assassins with ice water in their veins. Accept that and move on. Understand the things that really drive change. Capitalize on creativity and innovation. Go that extra mile!

The New Vehicle for Success

VI

"Nothing endures but change" - Heraclitus-540 B.C.

A historic shift has been created by you and your executive team. Employee morale and buy-in should be increasing every day. Where do you go from here? Don't forget the cardinal rule. **"There is no room in your organization for loyal, yet incompetent people."** Gardening must become a way of life. Continuous pruning will keep you on track as your team rises or falls to the occasion. If an assessment of the company and your team was performed properly, pruning will be a non-issue. If you made mistakes, pruning will become an active initiative.

Remember – Profit is NOT a Dirty Word

What we are facing (economic turbulence) is not at all unprecedented. Simply put, there are good times when things are going well and it's easy to make money, and there are bad times, when it's much more difficult to make money. Prior to 2008 we had a run of good times that exceeded most of our expectations. I have often said that it didn't take a genius to make money during that run.

However, "Profit covers many sins." That means that many of us got a little complacent. Maybe we didn't quite run our business following absolute best practice. Maybe some of us overlooked less than the best performance expected from our employees. Maybe we were a little too compassionate regarding employee effectiveness and as a result we haven't "weeded the garden" to allow our good employees to flourish.

Walk the Walk

By now your gut should be telling you if your team, your company, can now **walk the walk.** Confidence in execution means you are on the winning side of turmoil and confusion. You have created a vehicle that can take you where you want to go. More importantly, you know how to get there. You now have the vehicle, the process, the initiative and the team to execute. This vehicle has provided the following:

- A clear plan with clarity of purpose and participation of the employees
- A raised bar with relevant accountability
- A definitive marketing and sales strategy
- Best practices and determination to reside in the upper quartile for performance once recovery is secure

The New Vehicle for Success

- A measurement of success through activity management and customer satisfaction formally

You are now in a position to execute your initiatives. You attacked your sales process first. The sales process is at the heart of your success. Labor costs and executive effort invested in this process during your recovery often exceed 25% of your total gross margin dollars. It is both complex and subjective because it deals with both customer management relationship activities and contingency-recovery initiatives.

You have asked and answered the following questions in creating the vehicle you intend to ride to success. You must take action based on those answers.

- What determines a profitable customer?
- What methods and processes do you use to identify customers?
- What is new in the external environment?
- What are your competitive advantages?
- What are your competitor's competitive advantages?
- What are the methods used for gathering competitive intelligence?
- What changes have taken place externally or with your competitors that offer opportunity?
- What initiatives do you have to improve highest delivered value?
- What initiatives do you have to reach the goal of low cost provider?
- What types of customers and segments do you want to do business with?
- Who decides what customers you target?
- What types of customers are the most profitable?
- Have you identified target markets?
- How do your sales representatives spend their time?
- How often do you plan formal business reviews to compare expectations to results?
- How do you measure costs?
- Who reviews and is responsible for customer profitability?

- How do you measure customer retention?
- How do you track lost business and lost customers?
- How do you determine which customers to fire?
- How do you prospect?
- How do you identify critical success factors?
- How many and which customers represent 80% of your revenue, your profit?
- Has your average order size increased or decreased?
- What single thing has the biggest impact on your profitability?
- What are your competitive strengths?
- What volume does the top 10% of your customers represent?
- What do your sales representatives claim the key obstacles to their success are?
- What support could be added to your sales effort to increase revenue producing actions?
- What is your current market share?
- How do you measure growth?
- How do you maximize account penetration?
- What is the role of your inside sales staff?
- Do inside sales proactively solicit business?
- How do you define supplier performance?
- How do you forecast usage?
- How do you analyze your warehouse operations?
- What are your inventory turns?
- Do you measure your cash to cash cycle?
- What metrics are you using for supplier performance?
- Have you defined and analyzed your logistics initiatives?

Competitive Analysis – Don't Take it for Granted

I still remember the days when I was extremely active in organized sports. I'm talking about baseball, football and, yes, I even played soccer. Today, my mind still thinks I could play like I did when I was 25 years old but my body disagrees. Consequently, my total sports activity today is golf and pickleball.

The point I'm getting at is simply how athletes prepare for a competition. The very first thing they do is study the competition. I mean really figure out exactly who they are going up against. They know their opponent's statistics, their records and most importantly they study both their strengths and their weaknesses. Doesn't that make sense? Really, if you plan on being better than your competition, the more you know about them the better chance you have of defeating them. Now, if you agree with this concept, doesn't it make sense that the very same principles apply in the business environment? Let's face it, even Tiger Woods studies his competition and golf is much more of an individual sport where the competition is often the course itself.

A Key Component of Your Planning

When I am working with companies in the development of their contingency planning or strategic planning it is essential to create a comprehensive competitive analysis. Most companies rarely take this as seriously as they should. Oh, they know who their competition is generally but rarely do they really understand their competitor's strengths and weaknesses. More importantly, they often just guess at the competitions value propositions. This can lead to false assumptions or what I call "Cherished Beliefs." A cherished belief is something that is taken as fact but really has no data or information to validate the accuracy of the assumption. As an example many companies believe they demonstrate or strive for "World Class Service" when in fact compared to the competition it is often just average.

Competitive Analysis Starts with a Comparative Analysis

In order to create competitive advantage it is critical that you understand what value propositions your competition offers to your customers. The ability to get a potential customer to switch from your competition depends on their perceived value of your company, your product and you personally as compared to your competition. It's a simple concept:

"Perceived value drives customer expectations"
"Performance value drives customer satisfaction"

The higher you raise a customer's perceived value of you, your company and your products, the closer you come to creating competitive advantage. It's competitive advantage that will motivate customers to switch vendors and I am not referring to price. Be careful. Raise expectations so high that you can't perform and you shoot yourself in the foot.

Where Do You Start

The first place to start is on your competitor's website. It often amazes me how much information can be obtained simply by utilizing the Google search engine. Don't stop with just their website. Surf the net looking for any and all information you can find. Other good sources of information include both your customers and your vendors. Find out exactly how your services and value propositions stack up against theirs. When taking on this task, think of your customers Service Output Demands (SODS). Knowing exactly what the customers' expectations are will lead your research into determining exactly what the competition is offering. SODS can include but not be limited to the following:

- Terms
- Discounts -- Rebates
- Seasonal buying schedules
- Co-op advertising
- Packaging
- Quality
- Service and delivery including fill rates and on-time deliveries
- Inside and outside sales expectations on coverage
- Customer service preferences
- Product knowledge
- Technical support
- Warranties
- Returned goods polices
- Buy back- policy

Trust but Validate

It is difficult to build your competitive analysis strictly based on the opinions of your salespeople. You need to know what the reality of the situation is, because *that's* what you will be actually competing against. Utilize all resources and options to determine the reality of your competitors offerings compared to yours. This can be accomplished by using a variety of tools including:

- Customer focus groups
- Customer surveys
- Voice of the customer – phone interviews
- Outside sales feedback
- Inside sales feedback
- Internet research
- Executive feedback
- Historical data

- Competing salesperson interviews (This is opportunistic in that it only applies if you are interviewing to fill a sales position and a competitor's salesperson happens to apply).

Most businesses over-rate their customer service, without knowing what their competition actually does. This can prove to be a big mistake – especially in today's challenging economy!

Caution—Be careful with conversations with suppliers

Some conversations with suppliers, who also supply your competitors, can be of minimal value. Also, be extremely careful what you say to anyone who gives you too much information. Remember, they may be talking about you to your competition as well.

My Competitive Analysis is done….. Now What?

After researching your competitors, take a good close look at your own business and highlight both the differences that point out your weaknesses and the differences that point out your strengths. When it comes to your strengths, make sure your salespeople and your marketing is emphasizing the right message. As for the weaknesses, make it a priority to address each one of them to not only match your competition but to improve your position against your competition. Once you understand your competitive advantage (strengths) and you have addressed your weaknesses to turn them into strengths, take that message directly to your markets. You now have real competitive advantage and you can gain market share, increase revenue and improve profitability.

It's Time for Action

You have now answered many questions. You have immobilized the old culture, your contingency plan is complete; you may have restructured the organization. Hopefully you have reacted appropriately. You have defined your business functions. Now it's time to take **this "new vehicle" for success on a test run.** The new vehicle (The New Organization) is now made up of four distinct processes that communicate the new culture you are trying to create. The first and most important of these processes you have initiated is the change process.

The Change Process

The change process begins with the strategic restructuring of the organization, which was required to "Stop the Bleeding." This is generally a key component of your contingency plan. It will be concluded with the successful implementation of your long-term strategic plan (addressed in chapter VI). This process starts with the immobilization of the old culture. This is mandatory, as introduction of change into any existing culture is difficult at best. Introducing change into a losing or stagnant culture is almost impossible. Change must deal with organization theory, social psychology and business history. It must be dynamic and include the introduction of a fresh new leadership model built on trust and respect. This is a behavioral process. People can create change but people also resist change. The change process you introduce must answer the question, *"How do we get from here to there?"* The answer to that question is your new vehicle for success. This vehicle includes your restructuring plan, individual one-year business contingency recovery plans and every strategic initiative developed by your management team. Most importantly, this new vehicle is submerged in the empowerment theory releasing individual employee initiative. The plan must be unified, simple, consistent and universally understood by everyone.

The Differentiator

I often ask clients exactly what is it that makes them different from their competitors? The answers are wide ranging and include things like:

I Can Make a Difference!

- World class service
- Exceptional new product introduction
- Technology
- Experience
- Our Chinese connection
- Our design capabilities
- Our Pricing
- Operational excellence
- One – Stop – Shop
- Our logistics system
- Locations
- Our size

All these things are good. In fact some of them may even be classified as "Core Competencies." However, the answers I receive to that question are often disheartening to me. You see, rarely do I ever hear the answer;

"It's our employees that really make a difference."

Employees matter. Employees are the real differentiator. Think about it. I submit to you that every answer I listed above and any other answers that you may think of become important because it's your employees that create that success. World class service is not a core competence. It is what your employees do to create that level of service that becomes the core competence. They are the differentiator.

Your customers can buy from anyone; loyalty is an especially elusive factor during tough economic times. They have many choices. And, don't forget, your employees have choices as well. Some companies truly believe that their employees are their most important asset. Treat them like they are not and they may just choose not to work for you anymore. Often times when employees leave --- customers follow.

Lone Wolf – autocratic – insensitive leaders may not get it. Times have changed. New generations have entered the workforce. The number one priority of keeping your customer happy, although still paramount, has become the number two priority. The number one priority is keeping your employees happy. If you do that, number two becomes much easier. Effective leaders are driven by a model. A model is a tool used to predict future outcomes of current decisions. Effective leaders build their models on the sum of their experiences, knowledge and deeds as well as their mistakes. This truth is at the core of learning how to be a winner instead of a survivor. Recognition

Don't Be a Lone Wolf!

and praise raises self-esteem. Positive feedback and ample communication allow employees gratification and a newfound confidence in the organization. Command and control works for the military but leadership in the business environment must be built on dignity, trust and respect.

Richard L. Daft one of the country's recognized academic leadership experts raises the question, "What kind of people can lead an organization through major change?" Contingency planning and restructuring qualify as major change and require transformational leadership. Daft points out that this type of leader is characterized by the ability to bring about change through innovation and creativity. This type of leader motivates people to not only follow their lead but to believe in the vision of corporate transformation, the need for revitalization, to sign on for the new vision and to help institutionalize a new organizational process.

Principles of Effective Change Creation

As a leader you must implement change to create continuous improvement. It's a hands-on process. You can't lead from afar. A former colleague of mine used to always say; *"It's easy to be brave from a distance."* Arguably that may be one of the truest statements made when it comes to the instigation of change. Change is hard work. It requires process tools that are sensitive to your organizational culture. Consider these principles for managing change:

- Employees throughout your organization generally have the talent and the ability to be successful at meeting new challenges to growth and profitability.
- Employees understand change that is essential to achieve goals if those goals are clearly stated.
- Employees gain increased respect for leaders that become the architects of change. This is especially true if the leader encourages and solicits input from the employees.
- Leaders must systematically manage the change they create with fearless abandonment demonstrating a purposeful and disciplined approach that engages the entire organization through active participation in the success process.
- Employee ownership of change, the vision – end game and the strategic initiatives is one ingredient that is absolutely essential to success.

Change Can Take on Many Forms

MACHIAVELLI wrote in the forward to "The Prince":

"There is nothing more difficult to carry out, nor more doubtful of success, nor more dangerous to handle, than to initiate a new order of

things. For the reformer has enemies in all those who profit by the old order, and only lukewarm defenders in all those who would profit by the new order, this luke warmness arising partly from fear of their adversaries, who have the laws in their favor, and partly from the incredulity of mankind, who do not truly believe in anything new until they have actual experience of it."

Are You My Prince?

Effective leaders know that creating and managing change starts with the human side of the equation. Behavioral change becomes a necessity for almost every success initiative employed. This often means more effective coaching, training, skill development, and accountability. Process improvement is often a platform that supports change in the organization. And last but not least, change becomes a meaningful part of organizational structure and culture. This often requires a realignment of reporting relationships and responsibilities. From an organizational culture perspective, change may demand adjustments to some managerial styles, values and even belief systems to some degree. This is often the most challenging aspect of managing change. The leader may find himself facing the old cliché – "If you can't change the manager --- change the manager."

The organizational culture itself must embody a commitment for taking ownership of the contingency plan and raising the performance expectations is a matter of fact and not chance.

Induced Change vs Autonomous Change

Most of the change that has been introduced must be induced change versus autonomous change. Autonomous change has a life of its own. It happens because of internal dynamics and follows its own course. It is not easily controlled as it forms its own dynamics. Induced change is calculated and planned. It can be controlled if buy in is generated through sincere communication and employee involvement. Each step along this path will be accompanied by distinct challenges. As questions arise, management must be prepared to answer openly and honestly. While the old culture is suspended, change can thrive under the right circumstances. It is the responsibility of the executive team to ensure that these circumstances exist. The primary ingredients that create the right circumstances include open honest communication, empowerment, risk taking, acknowledgment and reward.

The Work Process

The work process is the engine of the new vehicle. This is how you are going to accomplish the objectives established in your Turn-A-Round or contingency plan. It involves measurement and accountability. It begins with a powerful idea.

Success will be created through hard work linked through chains of activities by different groups that synergistically unite into one cohesive effort with common objectives.

This activity is cross-functional and does not allow for silos or political agendas.

The work process involved will create, produce and deliver according to the specific stated objectives. Processes that do not deliver the desired output will be easily identifiable and must be corrected immediately. Both operational and administrative processes are included and must support each other. Their activities are linked even though they may be interdependent. Together they transform into cohesive outputs. The work process is probably the most familiar process to line managers. It relies heavily on the process of reengineering and quality. It is easily understood and unlike the change process, it is very tangible and measurable. It becomes recognizable that many prior processes may have gone unchecked with little rationale and planning. This creates inefficiencies.

Most processes in a work environment are not preplanned or designed. They just happen and no one pays attention or questions them. Consequently, redesign of most work processes is an essential part of the new vehicle for success. The redesign of work processes allows management the opportunity to address work fragmentation and encourage cross-functional integration. This also generates bench strength for future growth. This process also identifies new targets for improvement as manager's focus on the underlying process and not on structures or roles. Work process is only part of the new vehicle, the engine; success will not come with process redesign alone. Management, change, organization, recruitment, retention and strategic planning are all a part of the total package.

The Organizational Behavioral Process

Organizational behavior is basic to creating change, and it becomes an important part of the new vehicle for success. You may relate the behavioral process to the wheels of the new vehicle. This process will carry the organization on to new heights, new accomplishments. Organizational behavior has its roots in organizational theory and group dynamics. People are the most important ingredient to every organization and the organizations behavior. People and how they are treated will reflect the organizational characteristics; the way it acts and interacts with its own people.

"Employees won't start respecting you until YOU start respecting them."

"Employees won't start trusting you until YOU start trusting them."

An effective leader must be able to interact with employees, peers, superiors and many other individuals both inside and outside the organization. Leaders must gain the support of many people to meet or exceed established objectives. This means that they must develop or possess a unique understanding of people. The ability to coach-mentor and teach leadership skills to others is the driving force that will create effective organizational behavior. Being an effective leader requires the understanding of the principles that govern employee behavior. Accomplish that and success is imminent.

Changing out Management does *not* Guarantee Success

Empowerment, the decision making process and the communication channels are examples of how the organization interacts with its people. Organizational behavior is not easy to change. That is why it is as important, as mentioned in earlier chapters, to **immobilize the old culture to introduce change**. The behavioral process of the organization can withstand personnel changes. In other words, changing out management does not guarantee change in organizational behavior. You must take proactive steps designed to create new organizational behavior. The new vehicle is part of that. It includes, focused specific objectives, open channels of communication, empowerment and a sincere respect for the individual employee and their contribution to the organization.

The Leadership Process

Leadership is often described as the art of getting people to accomplish specific objectives. However, organizations are complex social entities with widely distributed responsibilities and assets. Unilateral action toward specific objectives is seldom sufficient in itself to create the kind of success required during economic crisis. Managers spend the majority of their day working with and managing the activities of many people. The challenges include how to get the organization moving in the desired direction; the direction that has been clearly stated by the contingency/restructuring plan and the new vehicle for success. How do they generate the allegiance required, the commitment necessary and the sacrifice desired to meet the new objectives?

The answer as discussed in chapter III is **Leadership**. Leadership is the key to harmonizing diverse group interest into a focus specific mode that supports the mechanics of implementation. The focus is on the way managers orchestrate activities and events and engage others in tasks so that the desired results are realized. Action is key and is implicitly equated to professional leadership. This skill is subjective and often artistic. It varies with every situation and every individual. I believe leadership skills can be enhanced and fine-tuned but a basic ingredient of humanistic understanding must exist to create a platform for leadership development.

Leaders are skilled in communication. They use that skill to gain influence. The key to their success however, is demonstrating integrity by matching what they say with what they do. Leaders get results. They make things happen. They continually advance a clear agenda, get others to buy in and move the organization to recovery; accomplishing specific objectives. They are explicit, consistent, concise and sincere. They generally have an abundance of charisma although I have seen many leaders gain success with a quieter influence. Leaders take charge and are not afraid of responsibility or risk. Most people want to follow them. A good leader develops openness, honesty, clarity of purpose and a sincere caring for the people they lead. They gain commitment and trust by demonstrating respect for the individual. They have a keen sense of understanding. They believe in their task, they understand the objectives, they communicate clearly and they honestly project the understanding that they need the efforts of everyone to succeed.

I was once asked; "Rick what exactly is the secret to success?"

Without a doubt, I answered, *"the secret to success is people."*

I answered that question fifteen years ago. If asked today, my reply would be the same, **People**. However, I would add that the second and third ingredient absolutely essential to success is, leadership and communication.

Strategic Planning

Strategic planning is a key process that adjusts an organization's direction in response to a changing environment. It supports the fundamental decisions and actions that shape and guide an organization. A sound strategic plan can help define and focus a company's efforts to move the company in the right direction, using the best methods. Strategic Planning becomes critical once a company survives economic crisis and is in the process of rebuilding and growing market share.

Do it Right

Ever take your management team on a retreat where you all sing motivational songs and exchanged high fives; sit around a camp fire and drink the same Kool-Aid? Did you walk away with tons of enthusiasm and fifty different initiatives? Looking back six months later, what did you actually accomplish? Not much?

Don't feel bad if that sounds familiar—it happens to a lot of well-intentioned organizations, both large and small. It's caused by the lack of a fundamental team skill involving five factors—focus, process, accountability, prioritization and execution.

Once you reach the point that it is time to consider a long-term strategic plan that means your short term Turn-A-Round survival or contingency plan has been effective. Your profitability has improved dramatically and it's now time to discover just how good you have become. A critical factor in developing a strategic plan is looking at the end game first. Just exactly what do you want your company to be when it grows up? Ask yourself the following questions in the perspective of five years into the future.

1. What markets will your company serve five years from now?
2. What products will you distribute?
3. Who are your primary competitors?
4. What are your strengths?
5. What are your competitor's strengths?
6. How has your marketing strategy changed?
7. What are your core competencies?
8. What is the size of your revenue stream?
9. How is your revenue stream segmented?

These are just a few sample questions. Don't stop there.

Strategic Planning Overview

Strategic planning is a management tool. It is used to help an organization clarify its future direction – to focus its energy and to help members of the organization work toward the same goals. The planning process adjusts the organization's direction in response to a changing environment. Strategic planning is a disciplined effort to support fundamental decisions and actions that shape and guide what an organization is, what it does and why it does it, with a focus on where it wants to go and how it is going to get there.

Discipline is a prerequisite to this process because it requires laser-like persistence to result in a productive strategic planning initiative. The process raises a sequence of questions that helps planners examine current reality, test assumptions, gather and incorporate information about the present and perform trend analysis on the future industry environment.

Fundamental decisions, actions and choices must be made in order to develop a plan that becomes a roadmap to the future. The plan is ultimately no more, and no less, than a set of decisions about what to do, why to do it, and how to do it. It has taken into consideration future scenarios, and participants have engaged in end-game analysis chain linking back to the present to create individual Strategic Implementation Plans (SIPs). No doubt, some organizational decisions and actions are more important than others – and that much of the strategy lies in the hands of the executive staff and ownership about what is most important to achieving organizational success.

Strategic thinking is the basis of strategic planning and leads to strategic management. Part of the end game analysis (a look into the future) involves asking-**"Do you understand your markets and other driving forces?"** Just as "activity based management" is the application of "activity based costing," "strategic management" is the application of "strategic thinking" and the implementation of the strategic plan.

Strategic management is absolutely critical in today's environment of channel evolution. Strategic management increases your odds for success at a much greater pace than doing nothing.

Doing nothing is not an option

Strategic planning involves anticipating the future environment, creating an end game analysis so the decisions are made in the present. This means that over time, the organization must regularly perform trend analysis in order to make the best decisions it can at any given point – it must manage, as well as plan, strategically.

Strategic planning is not a substitute for the exercise of judgment by leadership. Ultimately **"The buck stops somewhere."** The strategic planning process does not make the organization work – it can only support the sound judgment and reasoning skills that people bring to the organization. Strategic planning is a creative process, and the fresh insight arrived at during the process might very well alter past initiatives developed during the contingency planning process. Planning consumes resources, a precious commodity. As a process that eventually defines the direction and activities of the organization, it can be an overwhelming and daunting task. Despite the overwhelming nature of the process, the benefits of planning can far outweigh the hard work and pain involved in the process.

I cannot emphasize enough that the true value of a strategic plan is not in the document itself. It is in the process of creating it involving many employees from the bottom up. This empowers them to be more effective and better-informed leaders, managers and decision makers. The time devoted to the planning process varies from organization to organization and you must decide how much time you will devote to the kick off planning process meeting. This can vary from a two-day retreat or you can engage in an extended process. The organization will begin to realize benefits from the start. Fundamental benefits to the planning process include:

- A framework and a clearly defined direction with unified support
- A clear vision and purpose that is owned by all employees
- Commitment to the organization and its goals by the employees
- Set priorities that match company resources
- Trend analysis that creates confidence in the ability to take risks

Readiness Factors

The planning process is a major endeavor and timing is critical. There are certain organizational elements that must be in place in order to ensure that the planning process will provide the maximum benefit to the organization. You must clearly understand the organizations current state and readiness to engage in the planning process. There are a number of preparatory steps that should be concluded prior to launching the planning process. If you have gone through a contingency planning-recovery process, an internal honest-gut-check assessment has provided clarity of purpose. Additionally, as mentioned earlier, third party customer, vendor and employee surveys have been completed. Other preparatory steps include:

- A commitment on the part of executive management and ownership
- Resolution of all crisis, critical constraint issues
- Board of Directors (BOD) support
- A commitment of necessary resources
- A willingness to think outside the box and to look at new approaches to performing and evaluating the "business"
- A basic understanding of scenario planning

The key resources required for planning include staff time,

executive management time and finances (e.g., market research, consultants, etc.).

Staffing Demands Include:

- Collecting and analyzing data
- Scenario planning
- Engaging key stakeholders
- Gathering historical financial information, projecting future budgets and cash flow projections
- Analyzing options and consequences for potential organizational and program strategies
- End game analysis

Project management becomes critical to the strategic planning process. People have different expectations when they hear the word "planning." Everyone must understand and share the same set of expectations. It is recommended that one or two key staff members are skilled in project management or utilize performance management software. Committees are not conducive to the creation of documents and quick decision-making. They are more suited to producing feedback, ideas and suggestions. A strategic planning committee with performance management support is a tool that is used to focus the energies and responsibilities of the process. The planning committee and the project manager control the process, but the executive team shares the responsibility for decision-making.

A good project manager will facilitate the development of the work plan. It is an outline of the steps and activities that will take place during the planning process. The plan specifies the tasks, outcomes, resources to be expended and the people responsible in each phase of the process.

How do you get started?

If you have determined your readiness factors through assessment and you have performed the necessary preparatory research, then you are ready to launch the process.

The First Priority

The following items should become your first priority:

- Create a Planning Committee
- Assign a project manager
- Identify specific ongoing initiatives
- Clarify roles (who does what in the process)
- Identify any additional research or outside resources necessary to assist you during the process

The Second Priority

The second priority is to clarify your vision with ownership and the executive staff leading to the creation of your end game.

The "End Game" -- What Does That Mean?

The End Game is actually a Chess terminology used in the context of the end game strategy to win the game. It focuses on centralization of the king, the role of the pawns, the principle of weakness and the bishop's impact and that is as far as I will go with chess talk. I am not a chess player. However, the concept of the "End Game" in business is actually quite the same as

Strategy Requires Strategic Thinking

in chess, the point being --- how do we win the game?

The "End Game" in business is simply defining what winning the game in your business is really about. What does winning mean? If you have seen one end game, you have seen one end game. Every end game is different, unique to the business, unique to its creator. The end game can be as simple as a statement about the character and integrity of the business or as detailed and complex as defining individual business segment growth with specific financial goals outlined with attendant timelines.

Strategy Is What We Are Talking About

Contrary to the definition of End, the "End Game" is really the beginning, the beginning of long term strategic planning. Strategic planning is a management tool. It is used to help an organization clarify its future direction – to focus its energy, and to help members of the organization work toward the same goals. The planning process adjusts the organization's direction in response to a changing environment. Strategic planning is a disciplined effort to support fundamental decisions and actions that shape and guide what an organization is, what it does and why it does it, with a focus on where it wants to go and how it is going to get there.

The mission statement or core strategy statement must clarify and communicate the essence of the organization. Articulating the end game indicates your focus and your expectations; a core strategy statement or mission statement should contain:

- **Purpose** – why the organization exists and what it seeks to accomplish
- **Business** – the main method or activity through which the organization tries to fulfill this purpose
- **Values** – the principles or beliefs that guide an organization's members as they pursue the organization's purpose

- **Character – Integrity** – what your company stands for

The mission or core strategy statement summarizes the what, why and how much of an organization's objectives. *It presents an image of the character, the culture and the core values of the organization.*

The Third Priority

The third priority entails performing the SWOT analysis (strengths, weaknesses, opportunities and threats). Since during your recovery process, you established "The Real Deal," the SWOT analysis should be a cakewalk. A SWOT analysis, as explained in an earlier chapter, means obtaining current information about the organization's strengths, weaknesses and performance information that will highlight the critical issues that the organization faces. These become key issues the strategic plan must address. These could include a variety of primary concerns, such as funding issues, new program opportunities, changing regulations or changing needs in the client population, and so on. The point is to choose the most important issues to address. Critical constraints should naturally emerge from this process.

SAMPLE   *SWOT ANALYSIS*

  Strengths: Brand Identities
           Strategically Located Branches
           Years of Industry Experience
           Multi-Cultural Ideas
           Centralized Distribution
           Branch Inter-linked Customer Support System
           Financial Strength
           Technical Capabilities
           Buying Power

Global Strength
Service Capability
Inventory Volume
Promotional Handouts and Brochures
Commitment to Education

Weaknesses: Morale
Stability in Manpower
Vendor Relations
Inventory Management
Education
Negative Buzz
Culture change has not been accepted
across the board
Bureaucratic Drag (Red Tape, response time)
Customer Service Levels
Freight Inefficiencies
Business Acumen of Sales force

Opportunities: Business Acumen of Sales force
Employee Recognition
Brand Label
Employee Skill Enhancement Training
Market Segment Development
Team Building (Internal/External)
Focused Innovation
Multiple Distribution (new suppliers)

Threats: Loss of Talent to Competition
Customer Service Levels
Vendor Instability
Market Segmentation

Pressure to meet short-term goals conflicts
with long-term plan
Regional Economic Issues
Integrated Supply
Multiple Distribution (Current Suppliers)
Effective Competition

Critical Constraints

Identifying Critical Constraints is the key objective when doing a SWOT analysis. You are looking for any type of challenge or roadblock that can derail the strategic planning process or any specific initiative within the strategy itself. The biggest mistake most strategic planning teams make in doing a SWOT analysis is the failure to identify constraints and develop actions to overcome them. Constraints may include things such as:

- Network Capabilities
- Inventory Management Issues
- Logistics Management Issues
- Customer Response Center (CRS) and Phone System Issues
- Training issues
- Staffing
- Technical issues

Critical constraints represent areas that are obstacles to obtaining objectives and goals. The management team must encourage and promote creativity and innovation from all our employees to ensure that these issues are transparent. The management team must empower the employees to make decisions that overcome weaknesses in these areas. This will be done in an effort to allow time for the company to improve the performance in the areas mentioned. It will also help identify areas of weaknesses by distributing non-conformance reports to the appropriate departments to ensure corrective actions will be taken. This will give employees the solid belief that they can make a difference.

The Fourth Priority

Getting back to the priorities; the fourth priority is to begin to develop departmental initiatives required to support the overall end game. Strategies, goals and objectives may come from individual inspiration, group discussion, and formal decision-making techniques and so on – but the bottom line is that, in the end, the leadership agrees on how to address the critical issues.

This can turn into a negotiating process and eat up considerable time and flexibility. It is possible that new insights will emerge which changes the thrust of the end game. It is important that planners are not afraid to go back to an earlier step in the process and take advantage of available information to create the best possible plan.

"Changing the End Game is not a crime."

The Fifth Priority

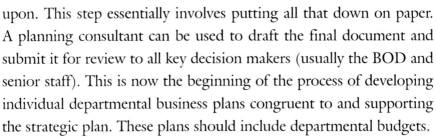

The fifth priority and conclusion to this abbreviated explanation of the process is producing the completed documented plan. The end game has been articulated, the issues identified and the goals and strategies agreed upon. This step essentially involves putting all that down on paper. A planning consultant can be used to draft the final document and submit it for review to all key decision makers (usually the BOD and senior staff). This is now the beginning of the process of developing individual departmental business plans congruent to and supporting the strategic plan. These plans should include departmental budgets.

Strategic planning involves looking at a longer time horizon, identifying future trends and developing action plans based on the highest probabilities. A good strategic planning process will enable a business to anticipate changing trends and implement actions that will enable them to gain or maintain competitive advantage. Acquiring strategic thinking skills is both an individual and a group effort. The bulk of the ideas come from reading other sources of information. However, the credibility and usefulness of this thinking emerges mainly after discussion refines it into relevant issues addressing future possibilities.

Academic Outline -----A typical academic outline of a strategic plan may look something like the following:

I.   The Executive Summary
II.   Company Description
III. Industry Analysis
IV.   Target Markets
V.   SWOT Analysis
VI.   Competitive Analysis
VII. Marketing Strategy
VIII. Sales Strategies
IX.   Operations Plan
X.   Management and Organization
XI.   Exit or Succession Plan
XII. Financials and Performa's
XIII. Appendix

EXECUTIVE SUMMARY

The executive summary is important because it provides a clear, concise and compelling condensed version of your business strategy as an introduction to the overall plan. It should be enticing and make the reader want to turn the pages to investigate your definitive vision and roadmap for success. The executive summary should be the last thing you create. After all, it is a synopsis of your overall plan. You can't possibly write it until your plan is completed. However, it should be the first thing presented in the very front of your documented strategy. This summary should include the following points:

- Your basic business concept explained in layman's terms
- Discussion of the planning effort
- Confirmation of capable management
- Clear cut market descriptions
- Your competitive advantage and core competencies
- Financial expectations

COMPANY DESCRIPTION

This is a simplistic description of your company outlining the Vision and Mission statement.

INDUSTRY ANALYSIS

This is an explanation of the external environment your company operates. Trends need to be discussed as well as strategic opportunities. Size, growth rate, market share, industry maturity, seasonality and any regulatory concerns all must be a part of this section. Distribution channels as well as e-business opportunities and threats are part of the discussion.

TARGET MARKETS

You must convey a thorough understanding of your customers and your customers' customers (referred to as C2). You need to be able to articulate a market assessment as to your customer needs, rules of engagements, what drives their value propositions and the logistics of satisfying those needs.

STRENGTHS, WEAKNESSES, OPPORTUNITIES AND THREATS (SWOT)

Simply put this is a gut check reality as to exactly what your business is all about. It is highly recommended that you don't stop at taking a personal parochial view of your company. An internal third party employee survey and analysis is recommended as well as an external customer and vendor survey analysis. This will allow a check and balance to the reality of your strengths, weaknesses, opportunities and threats.

COMPETITIVE ANALYSIS

This determines your real market knowledge. You must not only know the majority of your competition, you must understand their go-to market strategies. Know their strengths and weaknesses and build your plan to take advantage of that knowledge. Organic intelligence as well as external market analysis information can be used in your analysis.

MARKETING STRATEGY, OPERATIONS STRATEGY AND SALES STRATEGIES

This is documenting the major SIP's (strategic implementation plans) generated to accomplish your overall objectives. Included in these individual initiatives are the "critical constraints," "milestones," "timelines" and "accountability."

MANAGEMENT AND ORGANIZATION

This section covers your human resource strategies and outlines your organizational development. Individual executive profiles are included outlining the experience and expertise of your management team. A current organization chart and future organization chart should be included.

SUCCESSION PLAN

No strategic plan is complete without some form of exit

strategy. This can include succession, sale of the company, ESOP intentions or even taking the company public. Although this may be a topic with uncertain clarity, at a minimum different options need to be discussed. This is especially critical for privately held family owned businesses.

FINANCE

This section needs to have its own operational plan. That is as important as having a sales strategy or marketing strategy. This section determines how you are going to finance the business. It includes proforma's, which predict profitability based on the plans overall objectives. Cash flow analysis is a very important part of this section.

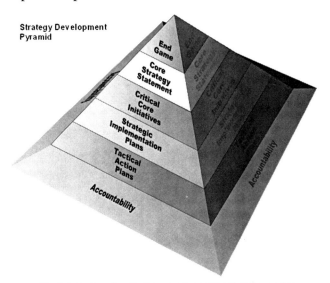

Strategic planning is a management tool. It is used to help an organization clarify its future direction.

This academic example does not mean every strategic plan has to follow a certain format, design or formula. The true value of a strategic plan is not in the document itself. The real value of a strategic plan is getting the employees involved from the bottom up in developing the plan. The experience, knowledge and buy -in gained during this process are invaluable. The format is not the most critical element. There is no exact way to document your plan. The importance is in the involvement of the people. Any format that conveys your strategy clearly, has built in accountability and has touched on all the issues mentioned in this chapter that are particularly meaningful in your industry is acceptable.

Sales Planning an Essential Offensive Strategy

VII

Whether you are in the contingency planning process, a restructuring process or you are in the recovery process and you have completed a strategic plan, the sales plan is the most critical component to success. A sales plan is a schedule of events and responsibilities that details the actions to be taken in order to accomplish the goals and objectives identified during the contingency – recovery – strategic planning process. The plan ensures everyone knows what needs to get done, coordinates their efforts and keeps close track of progress. Sales plans must define the objectives, timeline and resources required to meet the growth objectives of the business unit, department or branch. This level of detail is unnecessary in the overall initial planning process. The sales plan should now detail how the company will achieve growth, profit and product objectives. The sales plan is especially critical to the contingency or recovery planning process.

The basic sales planning process includes several elements:

- Individual territory plans outlining specific target accounts with attendant action plans identifying the steps necessary

to meet objectives
- Realistic forecasts
- A definition of services to be provided and the objectives quantified as revenue growth and profitability
- A commitment to timing and sequence of major steps
- An agreement to measurement criteria and targets
- Assigned accountability

Sales Initiatives should meet the following test. They should:

1. Be in Alignment with overall plan
2. Be Actionable
3. Focus on Market Share Growth
4. Focus on Margin Growth
5. Incorporate New Products/Services
6. Be Short term with Measureable Milestones
7. An Agreement to Measurement Criteria and Targets such as:
   - » Market Share Growth
   - » Margin Growth
   - » Company Growth in Revenue
   - » New Product or Service Sales
   - » New Account Development
   - » New Business Segments

Forecasting

Forecasting is an important part of the sales planning process as it becomes the platform for developing target account action plans. Historical data is essential to predictability but forecasting is exactly what the term suggests; predicting what is going to happen over the course of the next twelve months. This is a critical function of the planning process that is often taken much too lightly. Using the Pareto Rule, 20% of your customers will account for 80% of your business, is a good starting point. That 20% must be looked at closely. True potential must be examined at every account that makes up the 20%. The initial forecast starts with the sales representative but it is up to management or ownership to demand documented reasons for the numbers at each of the accounts that make up 80% of the business.

Action plans should include:

- Clearly defined objectives by product, by segment
- Clearly defined responsibilities of all employees involved in accomplishing the defined objectives
- Identified risks and opportunities
- A scorecard for achievement listing key indicators of success should be developed
- Regular monthly plan review meetings must be established

Once sales management has reviewed all the forecasts and the action plans submitted, it must be determined if current resources will allow achievement of the plan. In other words, if the plans indicate a 30% growth in market share with a fair amount of certainty then determination of resource allocation becomes significant. If the plan does not show enough growth to maintain acceptable profitability, then individual territory discussions must occur in search of ways to close the gap between the forecast and minimum acceptable levels of profitability. The following questions help determine this process:

- Have we adequately listed individual territory opportunities?
- Has our new business development program played a role in our forecast?
- Is the forecast too pessimistic or too optimistic?
- Can the individual sales representative and the regional manager justify the forecast with rational discussion and data?
- Can existing staff handle the increase or will we have to hire additional employees?
- Do we need to consider cost reductions including an additional RIF?
- Will current inventory levels support this growth or will we have to significantly increase our inventory investment?
- Will we require an increase in storage space or handling equipment?
- Are there any other capital expenditures necessary to support this increase?
- What other cost increases do we anticipate with this growth rate? (i.e. increased service costs, phone, fax and other administrative support costs)

Characteristics of an Effective Annual Sales Plan

There are three important characteristics to a good sales plan:

1. An appropriate level of detail – enough to guide the work, but not so much that it becomes overwhelming, confusing or unnecessarily constrains creativity
2. A format that allows for periodic reports on progress toward the specific goals and objectives
3. A structure that coincides with the corporate plan (Contingency – Strategic – Recovery) – the goal statements for the corporate

plan and the sales plan are one in the same

Just as monthly financial statements often present a budget for revenues and expenses and then report actual figures for a given time period, so should sales plans allow for the same type of comparison: the plan declares the "forecasted revenue" work in terms of goals and objectives for each targeted account and reports the actual progress on a monthly or, perhaps, quarterly basis. This budget-to-actual report gives a clear reading on how the territory is performing.

Targeting and Planning Concepts

Program Objective:

The primary purpose and benefit of targeting and planning is to become and remain focused on your corporate objectives. These objectives may center on growth, profitability or recovery. They include Target Accounts, Prospects and Long Term Accounts as well as identification of individual opportunities outside the boundaries of the preselected target accounts.

T.L.S.—Tier Level Selling ®

*Utilizing the T.L.S. -- 5 * 5 * 5 Concept -- A TGA Growth Strategy*

TARGET GROWTH ACCOUNT: (TGA) ---------SELECT FIVE

The territory manager submits five accounts that have a high potential for growth with a high probability for success. These accounts are approved by the branch/sales manager and become the focus of both the territory manager and the sales manager during a monthly review process. Individual sales and profit objectives are established for each of these accounts and agreed upon by both the account manager and the sales manager. They become part of the scorecard, and individual performances to goals are tracked monthly. Once the TGA account is selected it cannot be changed without formal branch/sales manager approval. TGA accounts are generally accounts that you are currently successful with but you have not realized maximum potential (you may or may not be currently considered Supplier of Choice).

LONG TERM ACCOUNTS (LTA) ---------SELECT FIVE

These can be accounts that you are currently doing a fair amount of business with but you are falling well short of the actual potential of that account or these can be accounts that you are doing a little business with that have tremendous potential but it is going to take serious effort, teamwork, commitment and time to realize the potential for growth.

PROSPECTS ---------SELECT FIVE

These are accounts that you are not doing business with at all but they have substantial potential. Be careful here. Do not include accounts that are really long term. These should be accounts that have high potential with a reasonable probability of success in developing this account into a customer within ninety days (these last five accounts are likely to revolve and although changing these accounts is okay, a discussion with the sales manager should be required).

Basic T.L.S. requirements

- Identify sales potential by product by account
- Identify sales revenue potential in dollars
- Estimate potential gross margin by account
- Write specific detailed action plans for each of the 15 accounts
- A Sales Scorecard

- Established a monthly Territory Opportunity Action-planning Discussion (T.O.A.D.)

Managing the Planning, Targeting and Goal Setting Process

As a Sales/Branch Manager, you have many competing priorities. One of the *most* important is the need to manage the sales functions. The Tier Level Selling ® program and the various activities which are part of it are intended to help you in these sales *management* tasks.

From a management perspective, the goal of the sales effectiveness process is to improve the quantity and quality of the sales efforts of the sales force. Its primary purpose is to provide focus-process and accountability that will enhance territory performance. This enhancement will lead to an increase in the sales, profitability and market share for each individual territory.

The idea of planning and goal setting is to provide focus on target accounts. These are the accounts with the most potential for growth. The 5 + 5 + 5 analogy (TGA, Prospect and Long Term Accounts) simply points you to the five largest accounts you have with the most growth potential without ignoring growth potential from Long Term Accounts that may require extended time and commitments to crack. Additionally, it allows you to focus on new account development by listing five Prospect Accounts that you currently do no business with. This doesn't mean you now only have fifteen accounts. You still must service your entire account base. These are just fifteen accounts that have high growth potential and have been identified to receive a proactive, aggressive focus for growth. You must still manage and develop the rest of your active assigned accounts.

Account Selection

Planning, Targeting and Goal Setting is intended to increase the focus of your sales effort on the kinds of specific activities that will lead to sales, margin and market share growth. Before these activities are precisely defined, the Sales Manager must review the 15 accounts selected by each sales representative. Selection must be based on unfilled "real potential." Sales representatives should explain their rationale for selection backed up by data justifying that selection. Most of the information/data necessary to back up this rationale can be obtained internally from your database.

Customer Profile

The customer profile is information about the "internal" workings of your customer. It includes everything from the company's history and ownership to its day-to-day ordering process. Your account managers may want to complete a customer profile for each of the 15 accounts selected. The customer profile components listed are **the tendons and the muscles**, the core of Planning, Targeting and Goal Setting. Each element becomes a building block in the program's foundation. Without good dialogue with your 5 + 5 + 5 accounts, securing the information necessary to formulate a meaningful plan becomes very difficult. To ensure maximum benefit from the information you collect, the questions asked and the answers given should be recorded in the narrative. This allows you to understand the subject and the answer. It reinforces your ability to understand the concept and the account.

How do we get the information needed?

- Analyze internal historical data
- Do outside research on your customer's industry
- Ask the customer directly
- Ask the customer's competitors (carefully)
- Talk to your customer's customers

The following are some ideas and guidelines for the types of information your account managers should look for when completing the customer profile.

General Company Information

This provides an important snapshot of the account. It tells you exactly what kind of company you are dealing with. Areas to explore include: when were they founded? How did they get started? Are they private or public? Is their family still involved in the business? Where are they headed? Do they have a strategic plan? What are their growth expectations? Are they involved in any mergers or acquisitions? Who are the principals of the company? What are their demographics as it relates to their market, their location? What is their current and forecasted revenue? How many locations and employees do they have? What is their sales and margin split between products and services, commercial -- residential? What is their financial condition and credit rating?

Buying Process

Do they buy based on forecast, material requirements planning (MRP) or build to order? What is their ordering practice? What is their ordering lead time from their customer? By understanding their process, you can better determine the pain factors and the opportunities to become a total solution provider.

Vendor Practices

Are they implementing a vendor reduction program or any other type of program that has significant impact on their purchasing practices? What kinds of buyer programs do they have? Do they pay their bills on time? Are there any special terms required? What do they look for in a vendor? What do they think of you? Who are your major competitors for this account and what are they doing to win the business?

Critical Needs and Issues

What components are deemed to be highly critical in the customer's operation? What if anything has the customer done in the way of preparedness in case of breakdowns or business interruption? What about cost reduction, E-business, productivity, service and logistics? Describe major current initiatives that could affect the relationship. Examples could include vendor reduction, process re-engineering, supply chain projects, technology changes, and acquisitions. Look for the customer's pain. These are suggested questions to get you thinking. Don't stop there; be creative. The more you know about your target account, the better prepared you will be to shorten the time required to meet your objectives.

The Sales Scorecard – An Effective Tool

A primary source of performance measurement is the sales scorecard. So, if you don't have one, create one. A scorecard is nothing more than a summary of actual performance against identified targets and the objectives set for those targets. A territory discussion with individual sales representatives is the foundation to make scorecard utilization successful. These discussions should generally begin with a quick look at each measurement, along with the trends the numbers indicate. The scorecard should provide a checklist for territory progress and a review of action plans for each target account. If action plan tasks are being completed but the corresponding growth of the account is subpar, the sales manager and territory manager should discuss the reasons and consider changes to the plan and/or account goals. If the territory manager is consistently failing to complete action items on time, a discussion about time management may be warranted. The territory manager and sales manager should also verify that the specific commitments made at prior territory review sessions have been fulfilled. It is critical that both the territory manager and the sales manager have a clear, shared understanding of territory performance.

The Format

A basic sales scorecard may include but not be limited to the following:

- Sales revenue growth goals
- Margin growth goals
- New account development
- Individual target growth account goals (TGA's)
- Individual product or vendor goals
- Penetration goals

Personal Scorecard	Last full month		YTD	
	Goal	Relative Position	Goal	Relative Position
Consolidated Performance Score (CPS)	100%	90%	90%	90%
Sales vs. Plan	100%	90%	100%	85%
GP vs. Plan	100%	90%	100%	90%
Target Account Growth	$20K	110%	$200K	105%
Prospect Growth	$10k	90%	$100k	60%
Asgn Acct Growth	$15k	110%	175k	102%
Preferred Vendor Growth	$10K	90%	$75K	80%
Preferred Product Growth	$5k	100%	60k	90%
Other specific goals	$5K	90%	$5K	90%

Scorecard Sample

Sales Planning Tools
The Fair Share Analysis

Let's face it, the real opportunity and the easiest path to growth is through deeper penetration at those customers that are already doing business with your company. Common sense should tell you that if the customer is doing business with you then you have already established some sort of relationship with them. The question then becomes; are you getting the maximum share of their spend? Have you leveraged your relationship to the point that you are at least getting a fair share of the customer's spend? Although the following exercise may not be an exact science, it can at the very least provide some insight about your individual performance at your top twenty five accounts. Chances are very good, using the 80/20 rule that these twenty five accounts may represent eighty percent of your total sales. If that is not the case you can always add a few to your list. Don't ignore accounts that you know have tremendous potential but you just aren't getting much of it at all. These could become LTA's (Long Term Accounts).

So, just exactly what is your fair share of the customers spend? Most sales people would say; "That's an easy question -- I want all of it." But, let's be realistic and use the following guide to establish some targets and goals for increased penetration. It's called a "Fair Share Analysis."

Using the "Fair Share Analysis Guide" to Increase Account Penetration

Review the following table to understand how to figure your fair share analysis. There's potential for growth at most of your accounts. Completing this exercise will provide some focus and show you where you under penetrate. These are your target growth accounts

Customer	Sales	Potential	Actual Share	Fair Share Volume	Increase
A	$125,380	$230,000	54.5%	$78,200	----
F	$45,898	$200,000	22.9%	$68,000	$22,102
K	$27,568	$30,000	91.9%	$10,200	----
P	$13,971	$200,000	7.0%	$68,000	$54,029
U	$9,996	$250,000	4.0%	$85,000	$75,004

(TGA's) if the volume is there; it may also show you who you should eliminate.

List your top twenty five customers in descending order based on their total prior year's revenue. In column two list the potential of that customer to buy all the products you can supply. This is their total potential. Don't count revenue for products that you don't stock. Column three is simply column 1 divided by column 2 giving you your percentage of participation in their business. Your next step is to total column number one and column number two. Divide the total of column number one (the revenue of all top twenty five accounts) by the total of column number two (the total of all potential sales to the top twenty five accounts). This equals your *average actual share* of revenue spend for all your top accounts. In the example below, the average actual share of revenue is 34% (consider this your fair share bogey). Your next step is to calculate your fair share volume for each account based on your total average share. In some cases you will be doing more than the average. For customer A, your fair share based on the 34% average would only be $78,200 and you are actually doing $125,380. This shows a likely hood that there isn't great potential and probability to increase your penetration at this account. However, look at customer U. This customer has a potential of $250,000 and you are only getting $9,996 showing a potential for further penetration based on your average fair share analysis of 34% to be $75,004. *Note: All these tools should be used on a territorial basis. E-mail rick@ceostrategist.com to request this excel spreadsheet for calculations.*

The 10 X 10 Matrix

The 10 X 10 Matrix is another tool to help you determine which target accounts may have the highest probability of success. The idea of this exercise is to list your top ten

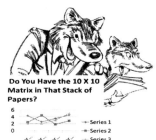

customers in the vertical column based on their total *Sales Potential for Growth*. Obviously you could do this exercise simply listing your top ten customers by total volume but I believe you will get better results on increasing your business if you consider your top ten based on potential for growth and not current revenue.

The horizontal column is used to list your top ten products that you represent. This list can be based on volume, profitability or preferred vendors. This is up to you and your specific objectives for each territory.

Fill each of the 100 boxes with:
(Y) Yes they use it & buy it from us
(-) They have no need for the product
(N) They use it but buy it from someone else
(?) Don't really know

Allocate resources to the N'S

10 X10 Matrix

BY TERRITORY: DATE:

10 LARGEST CUSTOMERS IN THE TERRITORY	1	2	3	4	5	6	7	8	9	10	TOTAL N'S

TOTAL N'S

The exercise is self explanatory. Put a **"Y" in the box** if your customers use the product and they currently buy it from you. Put a **"-"in the box** if they have no need for the product. Put an **"N" in the box** if they buy the product but they don't buy it or buy very little of it from you. Put a **"?" in the box** if you have no idea. However, this should alert you to the fact that you don't know enough about your customer and should do more homework.

Add up your total number of "N's" and allocate your time and resources accordingly.

The Probability Profile—A Simple Intuitive Calculation

The probability profile is designed to help you determine the probability of success at specific target accounts. The questions

Probability Profile

Award from 1 to 10 points based on the strength of the factor being present	
Factor To Consider	Points
The customer uses much of our product offering	
Something has changed	
Something is going to change	
Other (Documented Cost Savings):	
Current Competitor has personnel changes	
We have good personal Chemistry	
Total	

shown are just suggestions. You may want to add one or two that is specific to your industry, segment or territorial specifics. The idea is to allocate points to a specific account based on specific factors. The point total between one and ten for each question is based simply on your experience and intuitive judgment as to how that factor may help change the customers buying decisions. This exercise should be performed on all your specific TGA accounts. The value of this exercise is much greater when used as a supporting factor in conjunction with the other sales tools versus using it as a standalone exercise.

By utilizing all these tools, it allows you to validate exactly who your target accounts should be. This is simply intuitive based common sense backed up by the exercises you have completed using these tools. You now have a much better idea on how and where to spend your time and resources.

Don't be a "Lone Wolf"---- Use all Your Company Resources and Support.

Summary Criteria

Customer	Prior Year Sales	Our Share	Potential Increase	# of ns in 10 X 10	Profile Points

From here on, it is experience based intuition
Pick 3 – 4 Targets for full court press

Creating an Effective Sales-Management Program

To be truly effective and follow best practice involves focus, process, discipline and accountability. The sales team consists of all the individuals involved in the sales/marketing channel that serves the end user. Ideally, it should be a coordinated network, with strong alignment of individual activities with focus on objectives, process for continuous improvement, discipline toward utilizing best practice throughout the sales process and accountability for performance at all levels. Treating customers as partners, rather than customers, means that you must be interested in what they are selling, and how they make money; not just how much they buy. Your sales objectives must be in alignment with corporate objectives and your customer's objectives.

Creating an effective sales process includes planning sales growth, profiling targeted accounts, executing account strategies and using objective feedback to continuously improve performance and drive accountability. Creating this process supports a structure and mechanism by which this network can be managed as an integrated whole. It consists of processes, measurements, training and tools to improve the sales performance of the selling team. The processes and measurements create discipline so that the training and tools are actually used and performance is continuously improved.

The secret is simple but often misunderstood. The secret behind effective sales management is simple: manage activities and measure results. Sounds easy but the misunderstanding lies in the fact that the link between activities and results is very short in demand fulfillment functions (entering customer orders today means shipping more orders today and tomorrow). However, that link for demand creation is much longer and tedious. It involves strategic selling, building relationship equity and the creation of T.L.S. penetration strategies (relationships take months or longer to deliver revenue). In demand creation, attempting to manage results is like watering a plant after it has died from dehydration, because the current results were determined by activities performed months in the past. The only way to create an effective sales process is to define the activities that will drive results and then manage those activities.

Define Goals

Now that your account managers have selected their targets and collected critical information about them, it's time to quantify your goals. For each target account, your account managers should now create a sales target. The first item to be considered is exactly where you stand as a supplier or potential supplier right now. See "Fair Share Analysis." Your account managers should forecast both revenue and gross margin, by product and by quarter. This is not "pie in the sky" guessing. They should be able to back up their forecast with solid data and a reasonable thought process to the degree of your anticipated success. In other words, why and how do they feel they can accomplish this goal?

Action Planning

The final component of successful growth and execution is to document individual action plans to succeed at each target account. Your action plan should develop naturally from

Climb Out of the Turbulent Economic Hole by Creating an Effective Sales Plan

the knowledge you gain from your research and customer contact. You should develop one plan for each of the fifteen Target Growth Accounts. This plan must determine how to match your company resources to every opportunity that exists within that account. This action plan should encompass the entire year, a twelve-month period, with time lines, action requirements and accountability by assigned responsibility. Keep it manageable. Make sure you have the resources to accomplish each specific assigned task and the time necessary to deliver what you promise. Details are essential for every step. Clearly defined goals containing specific action items with assigned responsibility and accountability are a must. Each participant in the plan must acknowledge and accept responsibility for their portion of the plan. Definitive action plans are more than personal account visits once a month. They are more than introductions to upper management and they are more than a commitment to work with management to submit the lowest bid. Action plans must be precise, definitive and measurable. You start by establishing specific objectives for each target account and continue with objectives for each personal contact. You must identify specific participants necessary to meet objectives and develop strategies to accomplish those objectives. Each plan should address the questions, Who, How, When, Why and What For. Who should call on whom, etc? Develop entertainment strategies where necessary.

Territory Opportunity Action Planning Discussion (T.O.A.D.)

The T.O.A.D. is the most important component of the T.L.S. ® program. Critical performance issues are discussed during the T.O.A.D. It provides the forum for Branch/Sales Management and the Territory Manager to discuss, plan, and measure success. These discussions introduce accountability and identify opportunities for improvements with action planning specific to each objective. It is the Sales Manager's job to not simply participate in this process, but to use these opportunities to coach, counsel, and correct issues regarding performance. If conducted properly, the T.O.A.D. process will become an effective tool in improving both the Sales Manager's and Territory Manager's performances.

The only purpose of the monthly T.O.A.D. is to improve territory performance. T.O.A.D. should not include any activities that do not directly support this goal. If the Territory Manager does not find the review helpful, it has not served its purpose.

These sessions are not intended to be disciplinary in nature. They support rather than replace the existing annual performance appraisals. Remember, you are primarily reviewing territory performance, not individual performance, although the two are obviously linked.

Success Tips

SALES MANAGEMENT RESPONSIBILITIES

A Sales Managers Responsibility Does Not Focus on Selling but it Does Focus on the Promotion of Sales

1. <u>Developing the Sales Strategy</u> - Creating a discipline within the sales force to identify specific growth targets which include:
    - » Increased penetration of existing accounts
    - » New account development, pipeline management
    - » New product introduction and promotion

2. <u>Developing the Sales Force</u> - A key responsibility is self development and required leadership skills.
    - » Coaching and mentoring
    - » Providing training resources
    - » Hands on buddy calls
    - » Monthly territory/account discussions and review sessions (one on one) (See T.O.A.D.)
    - » Showroom management
    - » Policy and procedure enforcement
    - » Accountability

3. <u>Manage Activities – Measure Results</u> - Defining key activities and then managing those activities is a prerequisite to success.

    Design a sales effectiveness process that requires account action plan activities that include but are not limited to:
    - » Targeting
    - » Goal setting

» Opportunity reporting
» Pipeline management
» Performance scorecards

4. <u>Key Account Support</u> - The sales manager needs to develop relationship equity in conjunction with his outside sales person at all key accounts

Five Common Mistakes of Sales Management

1. **Lack of Structure** - Policies, procedures and the culture that determines the behavior and success of the sales force. Including:
   - How accounts and territories are assigned
   - Systems and procedure on walk in traffic
   - Compensation and SPIFF design
   - Confusing communication channel

2. **Lack of Strategy** - Effective documented sales growth strategy aligned with corporate initiatives.
   - Lack of growth initiatives that include penetration, new account and new product development
   - Acceptance of status quo without accountability
   - Excessive compassion and complacency

3. **Lack of Sales Effectiveness Process** - Process is the tendons and the muscles that link structure and strategy together. Process includes:
   - Targeting, goal setting and action planning
   - Monthly territory performance discussions (See T.O.A.D.)
   - Sales scorecards

- Coaching and Mentoring
- Effective sales meetings

4. Lack of Formalized Training and Development System Standards and benchmarks for performance for both outside and inside sales
   - Training Matrix with required support

5. **Wrong People** - According to statistics less, than 25% of top performing sales personnel promoted to Sales Manager are successful. Fifty five percent of people earning a living in sales should be doing something else. Twenty five percent of people with the ability to sell are selling the wrong things. (Herb Greenberg – *How To Hire and Develop Top Performers*)
   - Lack of formalized recruitment program
   - Lack of bench strength
   - Weak leadership skills

A Collection of Sales Tips across the Industry

- Meet and qualify all the accounts in your territory before you begin to focus on a few.
- <u>Do your homework</u>. Know your company first; the strong points, the weak points. Know who and what your internal resources are. What is your company's sweet spot?
- <u>Do your homework</u>. Know your customers. What do they buy? How do they buy? Who are their five largest customers? Research your customer and their industry on the web. Become an industry expert for your customer. Meet people and cultivate relationships beyond your customers purchasing department.

- Create a call plan prior to every call. The objective can be as simple as getting an appointment with someone higher up in management to meet with your management on a subject as complex as a full-blown PowerPoint presentation designed to secure a contract.
- Keep a data record on every buyer at your major accounts. Get to know them as well as their family knows them.
- Create an itinerary for each week. Know what you are going to do. Set at least two base appointments in the morning and afternoon with major accounts. Fill in around these appointments as appropriate.
- Know your customers' personality. People buy from people so develop a relationship with each of your customers. Personal Information Managers (PIMS) or sales programs such as TeleMagic and Goldmine have a place for this information. Use it, or put it in your spiral binder. Nothing is more important to Jennifer than her daughter's ballet or to Bill than his golf or his son's little league, **BUT** do not waste your time or theirs. Some people will reject you as a time waster if you talk about this, others will keep you on the phone for hours with trivia. Know your customer and control the conversation. Your job is to sell and move on but do it in the most productive and effective manner and only you know what that is for your customer.
- Create a territory plan. Establish goals, identify milestones, create a time line and engage all your resources including upper management.
- Create an action plan for every major account. Know your customers' "Rules of Engagement." What keeps them up at night? Create a strategy that involves your entire team including the President of your company if appropriate.

- Set specific goals and objectives. Write them down.
- Maintain a positive attitude. Don't procrastinate on anything.
- Keep your promises. Don't make promises you can't keep.
- Sell yourself first. Develop a trusted relationship, and then sell your company.
- Know your competitive advantages and your company's core competencies.
- Think creatively. Think outside the box.
- If voicemail is blocking your contact, call someone else's extension as if by mistake and ask them to transfer you. Voicemail has become the "gate keeper." Call early before business hours or later after business hours.

Listen more – speak less. Get your customer to talk about himself. If your customer spends most of the time in a sales call talking about himself, he can't help but like you. Apply the 80/20 rule – listen 80% of the time.

Is This Sales Plan Realistic and Achievable?

Survive Reorganization During Tough Economic Times

VIII

Organizations must implement change to offset economic challenges. It's a hands-on process that often requires total restructuring of the organization which invariably leads to a "Reduction in Force." Making sure you aren't one of the RIF's due to economic conditions is not an easy task. If you are one of the chosen that remain with the company, you are blessed. Keep in mind that the immediate aftermath of any restructuring based on contingency planning and economic conditions is very stressful and can be fraught with uncertainty. Try taking the following actions to improve your chances of survival while improving your productivity and reducing your level of stress:

- Don't wallow in guilt over friends that didn't make the cut. It is not your fault. Don't ask the question ---- Why Me? You need to focus and put forth your best efforts to make sure you stay on the team. You can't do that if you mope around in a cloud of self pity.
- Avoid contributing to grapevine gossip. Don't give management any reason to question your trustworthiness.

If you have questions or comments you want to share, do it privately with your immediate supervisor.

- Look for opportunity. Do you have skill sets that are underutilized or could be used in other areas that have never been tapped? Offer your services to management to help deal with the crisis.

- Don't try to place blame. Sometimes stuff happens. None of us are in control of the economy. If you believe the company was poorly managed keep it to yourself and work to improve conditions. Anger and resentment will not keep you on the team. If you are so adamant about poor leadership in the company then you should have left a long time ago. Now you have the opportunity.

- Become a champion of hope, change and an optimistic future. Control your attitude to ensure you project confidence in yourself and the company's ability to get through the crisis. Offset coworker doom and gloom with words of encouragement and optimism.

- Put a priority on developing your skills. Get additional training even if you pay for it yourself. Continue your education. Make yourself as valuable to the company as possible. Display multiple talents.

Don't wallow in self-pity. Commit yourself to success.

Remember… Surviving a restructuring isn't a gift. It just doesn't happen. You made the cut so pull yourself up from your bootstraps and commit yourself to your own personal success. Like the Wolf --- you must learn to lick your wounds. They will heal. Things will get better. Economic conditions will improve. But if you are going to ensure your own survival during the economic crisis, you have to plan for it. We all live 24 hours each day. What you do with that time determines your success. Ask yourself if you really have defined your own talents and more importantly, are you using that talent effectively? Are you doing your absolute best? Create a self-imposed respect for time. Learn to multi task. Treat time as an investment. *Believe in yourself, work hard, be committed and "Never – ever --- ever --- give up!"*

Don't Be a Procrastinator

"Procrastination is like a disease. It develops slowly, often over a long period of time."

It can be like an anchor around your neck. We have to learn to deal with it if we are to become effective at whatever we choose to do. You see, procrastination is the breeding ground for incompetence. If we don't learn to conquer it, we will never maximize our effectiveness and become everything we can be. Experts have written that only 20% of employees reach the level of effectiveness based on individual potential. I believe that procrastination contributes to that negative statistic. Procrastination can drain your energy, affect your attitude and suppress your creativity.

Five Common Excuses

These five common excuses are crutches. They are easy to site. Print these out and post them within eyesight to remind you they are what they are--- EXCUSES.

1. There's never enough time.
   "I don't buy it. You need to make time for the priorities you establish that lead to your success."

2. There are always so many distractions. Everything is urgent.
   "Learn to prioritize based on importance. Address things that are in alignment with your objectives."

3. I get tired of beating my head against the wall.
   "Don't lose your motivation, be persistent – don't give up. Success may be right around the corner."

4. What will my boss think? What will people say?
   "Learn to ask for forgiveness instead of permission. If you have thought things through, done adequate research, go for it."

5. Lack of confidence. It's better to do nothing than to make a mistake.
   "Believe in yourself. It isn't a crime to make a mistake. A mistake is one of the greatest learning tools known to man."

The key to success for anything you attempt is your ability to commit yourself with a passion. A commitment with a passion suggests you are someone who would rather take action and make things happen, than sit around and worry about what could happen. Without commitment you become someone who spends as much time avoiding the issue as others who just get it done. Procrastination is a waste of time and time is something you never get back once you spend it.

Leadership is about Taking Action

Leadership is often measured by your ability to take action. Yes, sometimes that means shooting from the hip by taking "calculated" risk. It becomes a function of how fast you can analyze a situation, take action and make things happen. The more proactive you are, the more productive you will become. This earns trust and respect. There is no greater reward than accomplishing a difficult task. However, you can't complete a project if it never gets started. Effective leadership deals with procrastination by applying the following tactics:

- Create self imposed deadlines to keep you focused. Don't create undo pressure but do make timeline commitments. Create milestone markers to judge your progress. These can be termed mini goals leading to your ultimate goal.

- Don't be a perfectionist. Unless you are a brain surgeon don't let perfection or analysis paralyze you into inaction. Sometimes good is good enough. The slogan "Good is the enemy of great" (Collins) does not apply when dealing with procrastination. Remember, once you decide on your initial actions you can always go back and adjust or react to circumstance. Remain flexible.

- Don't prioritize based on how difficult a problem is and leave it for last. Prioritize based on impact on your goals and importance. We face both easy and hard issues every day. Generally, it is better to get the tough ones out of the way first. Also, if you are in a leadership position, learn the art of empowerment and delegation. When confronted with a distressing problem or task, complete it immediately instead of wasting time avoiding it. This relieves your concerns, frees up your attention and allows you to move on to more productive activities. Taking on the easy tasks first allows us the opportunity to "lolly gag" in our actions to avoid the more difficult tasks.

Create a "To Do List"

My "To Do" List

I often wonder how many of you actually do "To Do" lists. I do "To Do" lists. I think they are basic to effective time management. I wouldn't have admitted this when I was younger but yesterday I did something that wasn't on my "To Do" list. So......... I wrote it on and then crossed it off. How many of you would admit to that? A "To Do" List will free up space in your mind so that you can concentrate on the job at hand. You can give these things your full attention without the stress of worrying that you will forget something.

Another thing I do that I wouldn't own up to when I was younger has to do with spelling. If I don't know how to spell a word, I'll write it real fast because I'd rather be considered sloppy than stupid.

Procrastination can become an immobilizer. Don't allow yourself to become susceptible to procrastination. Build up your defenses by striving to be proactive in everything you do. Taking action is always the best way to conquer procrastination. Doing nothing should never be an option.

Success During Recessionary Times

People who get results are high impact leaders. They are consistent, explicit and concise and they command a presence when they walk into a room. They have enough charisma to turn the dullest moment into a high-energy event. When they move on, others want to go with them. They have a following. Their openness and honesty create a legacy which people admire and look up to. They gain commitment and foster trust. Creating change, managing during turbulent times, or fostering growth in a recession all depends on a balance of this type of leadership. No one person can make a company successful. It takes a lot of people, but one person with a command of leadership can transfer enough influence, creating enough leadership amongst the management group to guarantee success. Most of us are not born leaders. We are not adept at communication. However, a good percentage of us long to become leaders and make deep connections in our careers that lead to commitment - a commitment to success.

To achieve our objectives we must understand the basic principles of leadership:

- Honesty

- Respect
- Trustworthiness
- Sincere concern of others
- Willingness to take calculated risk
- Becoming a Maverick
- Curiosity
- A sense of urgency

Once we have learned and practiced these principles we must learn to leverage our leadership skills to develop the management team around us. The true test of a successful leader is that he leaves behind the conviction, he leaves behind the will, and he leaves behind the understanding to carry on. Leaders must make emotional connections with the management team that surrounds them. They must encourage these managers to open up, share dialogue and reveal dreams. They must teach and mentor. Leveraging their leadership entails advancing their personal agenda by advancing the agenda of their management team. A good leader is not intimidated by the success of others. They encourage others to succeed and help them fulfill their wants and needs.

Leveraging leadership helps determine the hidden factors in communication. Understanding inferences and assertions becomes a key component to understanding people. Leaders have high questioning and interpretation skills that allow them to drill down to real facts and issues. Leveraging their leadership allows successful leaders to establish emotional connections, thereby diminishing fear and intimidation. This encourages enthusiasm and cooperation. Successful leaders take the time to listen, imagine and investigate numerous alternatives. With the involvement of people, they forge creative solutions to difficult problems. They meet the challenges imposed by recessionary times. They challenge their people to stretch, go beyond their previous boundaries and think outside the box. Successful leaders feed off their people and allow their people to feed off of them. They give credit where credit is due. They give recognition as a means of gaining respect. Through these methods they learn to create new insights and possibilities. Successful leadership means creating a sense of urgency and getting mutual commitment to action. Action steps are always clearly defined and precise. Often, due to the personification of the leader's own personality and charisma, employees are eager to leap into action - without forethought. High impact leaders communicate with encouraging clarity to command "buy-in" from every person involved to the commitments made.

Leading Through a Recession

The successful leader is constantly building advantages into the organizations with a sense of urgency while they are eliminating disadvantages. The belief is that you not only have to be better than your competition but you must differentiate yourself. This means taking advantage of opportunity presented by the economic downturn itself. This concept demands creativity and innovation. However, this creativity and innovation must be built into the economic contingency plan. It must be distinctive and yet it must be manageable and predictable. This could involve anything from new technologies to market segmentation to development of new channels to take advantage of the competition's weaknesses that may be accelerated due to the declining economy. It is all about improvement and finding newer and better ways of doing things. It involves cross-activity integration of processes and people. Activities must be linked across the entire value chain. Understanding the concept is critical to leadership success.

Manage the Cash

The primary focus of most organizations facing recessionary times is improved cash flow. Everyone has heard the cliché, "cash is king."

In a down economy, that becomes the most dominant issue about which leadership must be concerned. However, we must not ignore the fact that contingency planning cannot succeed in any organization without the revitalization of its people. And, revitalization of the people requires high impact leadership.

Cash to Cash Cycle

This cycle is extremely important. This measure illustrates how quickly a company can convert its products into cash through sales. The shorter the cycle, the more working capital a business generates, and the less it has to borrow. (E-mail rick@ceostrategist.com *if you would like an Excel cash to cash calculator.)*

Operational Definition

The cash to cash cycle is a continuous measure that is defined by adding the number of days of inventory to the number of days of receivables outstanding and then subtracting the number of days of payables outstanding. The result is the number of days of working capital the company has tied up in managing the supply chain.

Inventory Days of Supply

(Inventory $) / (Annualized COGS $ / 365) = Inventory Days of Supply

Days Sales Outstanding

(Receivables $) / (Annualized Revenue $ / 365) = Days Sales Outstanding

Days Payables Outstanding

(Payables $) / (Annualized Material Costs $ / 365) = Days Payables Outstanding

Contingency Planning May Lead to Survival Planning

If your organization finds itself in a financial crisis due to the economic decline, then survival planning becomes essential. This requires rapid analysis, quick decisions and immediate actions. This is undertaken with a deep sense of urgency. It creates a tidal wave of shock to the culture of the organization. Once this shock subsides, strong, high impact leadership must be present to set a course, structure an environment, and develop a team that can drive the organization back to success and profitability.

High impact leadership must be present during each phase of the contingency or restructuring process. Assessment, the first stage, is critical since leadership must not only capture a broad overview of the company to identify all potential problem areas for further analysis, but evaluation of management competency is a critical factor. *Often times, the reasons a company finds itself in financial distress can be traced directly back to the executive staff and past management practices. This becomes the platform for discovery of "The Real Deal."* There may be ownership issues. One or more of the executive staff may be at the core of the problem. This needs to be determined quickly and resolved with minimal emotion and maximum concern for the corporation's survival.

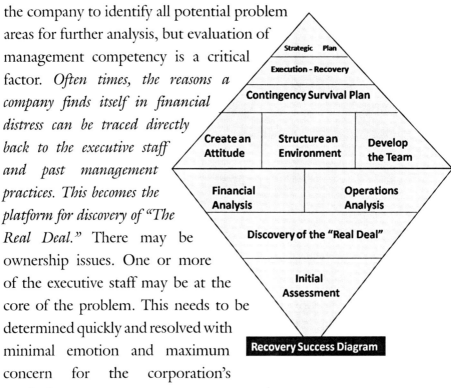

The other factors appearing in the success diagram demand that effective leadership is demonstrated throughout the organization during the entire process. **One person can't turn a company around.** Revising the organization chart doesn't turn a company around. Short- term plans, strategic initiatives and restructuring don't turn a company around. One person cannot deal with recessionary economics alone. One person cannot create growth. One person cannot create profit alone. People are not profit, but without people, teamwork and effective leadership, there are no profits. People create success during recessionary times - People who believe, people who are committed, people who care and people with values. You will find people with these traits in an organization that demonstrates high impact Executive Leadership; the kind of leadership that inspires people to get on board, be creative and innovative. The kind of leadership that creates an atmosphere of togetherness that perpetuates an aggressive approach to achieving common objectives.

Sales Success During Tough Economic Times

IX

A friend of mine was hired as President of a building supplies distributor in the Midwest. The company was profitable, but they seemed to have run into a brick wall once the economy started going south. This can be quite a challenge for any management team. It is not an uncommon problem. Sales in many companies may from time to time hit a brick wall and become stagnant regardless of the overall size of the company. My friend told me that his entire sales team seemed to have lost their passion. Their attitude resembled the cliché, "My glass is half empty."

Rekindle the Passion

Sounds easy but exactly how do you rekindle passion? Is there really such a thing as rekindling passion? The answer to that question is yes. Passion is a result of doing something you love to do. It means becoming really good at it. If you love doing it, you become committed to being successful at it.

You might scoff and say, "Rick, we had that passion in our sales force but this economy just puts a damper on it."

Not surprisingly, that does happen which brings us to the first question; how do you rekindle passion? I certainly can't downplay this. It is difficult. But, it starts with having the right sales leadership in place; a leader that has excellent people skills. Not sales skills but people skills, leadership skills that make people want to follow them. They make people want to release discretionary energy and give that extra. That may mean an extra call everyday or working till 5pm on Fridays or doing whatever it takes to provide solutions to customers problems.

If our Sales Manager has lost it, how do we get it back?

The answer to that question begins by asking yourself another question; do you have the right person in the job of sales manager? Are they a leader or were they simply your best salesperson? Do they have real leadership skills? Sometimes rejuvenating your sales force requires a change in leadership. It may even require a change in the sales force; the development of a documented sales strategy or even just a simple territorial restructuring.

However, before you get radical, ask yourself the following questions:

- Have you supplied leadership training for your sales manager?
- Have you provided any coaching or mentoring to support the sales managers' efforts?
- Do you get involved in supporting the sales strategy?
- Does your human resource department support a formalized program for new sales recruits?
- Do you show participative support in quarterly or semiannual sales meetings?
- Is the sales force held accountable – do they have scorecards?

- Is the sales manager held accountable beyond what I call the statistical disappointment review via e-mail?
- Is your sales force trained in value selling?
- Do they really understand what it means to be a total solution provider?
- Are they *targeting key accounts* based on potential for growth?

Nowadays, salespeople must be problem solvers able to generate solutions for customers in their time of need. Therefore, they must possess a great deal of knowledge about your customers' business. They must actually define what those needs are because the customer may not know, nor take the time to explain if they do

Target Key Accounts based on Potential

know. Customers want you to have the knowledge and intelligence to comprehend and analyze their problems before showing up at the door. Customers will listen and buy from the salesperson that finds the "pain" and takes it away. Sometimes going back to the basics is part of the answer to rekindling the passion. That means revisiting best practice in all areas including targeting, goal setting, customer profiling and action planning. Some of your salespeople may have forgotten and some of them may have never known the principles

Selling is a Profession that Requires Professional Leadership

Managing a group of professionals with the type of personalities required to succeed in sales is no easy task. This is especially true during tough economic times. So if you have done everything possible to support, educate and train your sales manager and you just can't rekindle that passion, you may have to change sales managers.

Sales management holds the key to meeting company objectives.

Effective sales management must build the platform for success. Salespeople are not the easiest group in the company to manage. If they were they would not be salespeople. Selling is not easy. It takes a special talent, self motivation, self discipline, a passion to succeed and the ability to accept rejection. The reality of the situation is simple. The majority of salespeople are not managed well. Today our sales environment leans toward a more multifaceted atmosphere; salespeople must become strategists with a plan. This plan requires more knowledge about the business, better relationships and better solutions. Some old school (Lone wolf) salespeople may believe they know what it takes. They have the experience. They've been around a long time. They also may have lost that passion. The world has changed. To rekindle the passion that has been lost may mean doing things differently. You can't afford to be complacent. Complacency destroys passion.

Sales is a Profession that Requires Professional Salespeople

Every company needs aggressive, creative and resourceful salespeople to have their products specified, accepted and used by customers. Without informed and capable field salespeople, no company could hope to compete when the economy is recessionary. But they have to have a passion for success and a leader they look up to that shares that passion for success.

I personally believe that good salespeople, the kind who can help a company really grow, don't just happen to come along by chance or fate. Just as some people believe there is no such thing as a "born leader;" I believe there is no such thing as a *"born salesperson,"* because selling ability is much more than an intangible given that a person either has or doesn't have. Granted, selling does require certain attributes in a person and some people are naturally born with these attributes and some aren't. Also, the person must be intelligent, able to grasp ideas and details easily, retain them and recall them for use whenever necessary in selling situations. These factors and many others relating to personal and emotional characteristics are contributing elements in the makeup of the professional salesperson. However, these attributes alone do not make a salesperson nor do they guarantee success. It takes more than that. A salesperson must also have a leader they can look up to, a leader they can respect, and a leader that can rekindle their personal passion when the tank starts to run dry.

So, if your sales people have become discouraged and unmotivated check the passion level of your team. Get involved with your sales force. Analyze what you have done as a company to support sales leadership. Become a coach, a mentor and take on the responsibility for rekindling that passion even if it means creating change.

The Service Factor During Economic Turbulence

The primary focus of your company's operations should always be on having uniformly excellent customer service. However, service excellence is mandatory during turbulent economic times. I define customer service as "doing what you say you will do." This involves setting customer expectations and then delivering on them. When the "fish were jumping in the boat," you could get away with less than world class service. Today, anything less than service excellence is just not acceptable. Improving and maintaining good customer service is not an exciting endeavor. It involves detailed study and steadfast execution rather than temporary brilliance or inspiration. Therefore, customer service improvement is fundamentally an effort of continuous improvement. You must develop a basic competency in process improvement to attain and sustain high levels of customer service. This means that it is absolutely critical during tough economic times that you don't make the mistake of cutting resources that support service excellence in your attempt to control operational costs.

Identifying Core Problems

It is strongly recommended that you create a detailed, documented process flow of what really happens in the realm of customer service expectations. This requires "walking through" the actual processes and asking a lot of questions. It's common for direct managers to have an idea about how a process *should* work without really understanding how it *actually* works. Often, a clear description of the real process makes the problem (or solution) almost obvious. When you identify a bottleneck try to trace back from the bottleneck to find the underlying or "core" problem. This simple technique helps you avoid treating symptoms instead of actual causes. For example, slow payments by your customers may be traced to invoicing errors, which in turn may be caused by incorrect pricing when the order is taken, which, finally, is the result of poor pricing guidelines. Often, the most fundamental cause of an operational problem involves organizational or emotional barriers rather than technical or procedural ones. Profit covers many sins; sins that may have been ignored when the fish were jumping in the boat.

Prioritizing Improvements

After you've identified a set of candidates for improvement it is tempting to attack many of them at once. However, experience shows that attempting to address more than a few major problem areas at the same time can be ineffective and even counterproductive. Most organizations don't have extra staff just waiting around for more work; especially the very talented people that you need to tackle a new initiative. This is especially true during tough economic times which may have dictated a reduction in force. This means that any new initiative <u>will</u> detract from your day-to-day business or other concurrent initiatives. Finally, companies often find that, after correcting primary problems, the secondary problems are completely different from those identified in the original analysis.

Designing Solutions

There are a variety of sound methods for designing solutions to operational problems. As stated earlier, the single most important element of solution design is to clearly define the underlying problem. It usually helps to state the problem or issue in a single sentence so that your entire project team has the same level of clarity on the issue. Four of the most useful methods are *brainstorming, best practices, streamlining principles and benchmarking*.

Brainstorming is a way of leveraging the creativity of a team to get better ideas. It is most powerful when the following guidelines are followed:

- Use a knowledgeable facilitator who is not directly involved in the process being discussed.
- Create a list of different considerations or aspects of the problem to stimulate thinking.
- Allow no criticism (even mild or joking) of any input. There are no bad ideas.
- Let ideas build on each other – this is the power of the team participation.
- Take a short break after the idea generation session before proceeding with qualifying the ideas. But be sure to qualify ideas during the same meeting into those which are clearly ineffective or undesirable, those which are clearly effective and desirable, and those which require further investigation.

Best Practice - Simply stated, "best practices" are business operations that are commonly used by financially successful companies. The identification and study of best practices is now widespread and has contributed to significant operational improvements in many industries. This powerful tool originated from a simple, almost obvious premise: at some level, most business organizations do the same things. Therefore, by examining those organizations that do these common processes extremely well, we can quickly find ways to improve our own business. Significantly, best practices offer a way to learn from any organization in any industry, provided that both organizations share a "common process." Here are some guidelines to using best practices effectively:

Remember that they are only correlated with good performance – be sure to use them as ideas for solutions rather than relying on them to fix problems that are specific to your company.

Good sources for best practices include the industry press, trade associations, peers in other markets, information from suppliers and customers, and general business literature.

Never blindly adopt a practice, even from a direct competitor, until you know exactly how it will work in your organization.

Streamlining (Process Reengineering) can often help you discover process improvements. Streamlining refers to the act of removing steps and time from business processes. Because time usually equates to money, streamlining can often lead to significant bottom line improvements. The following are a summary of these principles:

- Document the way the process really happens, not the way it should happen.
- Evaluate every step in a process to see if it is really necessary.
- Avoid unnecessary hand-offs between people. This is typically a large source of error.
- When in doubt choose error reduction over speed. It is estimated that over 25% of the labor cost in the distribution industry is involved in correcting errors.
- Attempt to do steps in parallel (at the same time) rather

than sequentially.

- Reduce variability processing time – even if all steps have the same average processing time, variability will always reduce overall throughput.

Benchmarking is a simple concept that is too often overlooked. Tremendous insight and problem solving ideas can be generated solely by observing how someone else runs a similar business to yours. Benchmarking involves searching for the best way to perform specific tasks in all functional areas. It is all about trying to become the best of the best and employ best practices that can generally be observed at those companies that perform in the upper quartile of performance.

However, benchmarking can be valuable regardless of how the company you are benchmarking performs. Even observing less than effective functional performance can teach us something and may in fact validate the things that you are doing right. Of course, benchmarking top performing companies is the ideal situation. Looking for companies that use different methods in accounting, customer service, sales, marketing, operations and inventory management can provide tremendous opportunity to evaluate your own processes and procedures for improvement methodology.

There are basically four types of benchmarking.

1. <u>Intercompany Benchmarking</u> – This process analyzes the top performance in key functional areas and looks at applying it to other functional areas.
2. <u>**Competitive Company Benchmarking**</u> – This is the study of a friendly competitor that allows you to come into their business and observe their practices. Generally this can be done with competitors that are not in your geographical service area. Keep in mind, it involves quid – pro – quo by allowing that competitor to observe your practices as well.

3. <u>**Similar Company Benchmarking**</u> – This is simply observing a company that is not a competitor but may be in a similar or related business. Although products may be different, systems, process and practices are often the same. This can provide insight for improvements in your business.

4. <u>**Functional Benchmarking**</u> – This type of benchmarking focuses more on a specific function such as "inventory management" among any and all companies anywhere that may be willing to allow you to observe and learn. The key is searching for the very best methods to excel in that particular functional area.

Benchmarking goals should be centered on making your company the absolute best it can be based on the top performance of other companies. Focus on targeting newer companies in your industry. Older companies often have an innate resistance to change, new ideas and new technology.

The Sky Isn't Falling

Many of you may assume that due to the current economic crisis business is going to be in the tank for a long time. Well, there may be some segments of **The Sky is Falling – The Sky is Falling!!!** business that take much longer to recover than most, but I still believe in our free enterprise system. I also believe that the market itself will make the corrections necessary whether the government intervenes with massive spending or not.

Some of you may be taking the attitude that now is the time to hunker down, cut costs and go into a cautious no risk taking mode while putting duct tape on your wallets and purses. Although I believe caution is prudent and contingency planning may be essential I'd like to stress that you shouldn't make blind assumptions and react too quickly without doing a complete analysis of your independent customer base and markets.

Economic Crisis often Presents Opportunity

Personally I believe that an economic downturn presents many opportunities to those companies that have diligently followed best practice and built a team of employees that can excel regardless of economic conditions. There is nothing wrong with controlling costs and being prudent. However, don't cut revenue producing positions, functions or systems. It is a proven fact that it is easier to gain market share in a down economy. I also think that now is the perfect time to invest in leadership skills training and manager training to strengthen the leadership skills in your company. Consider this:

Many companies panic during economic crisis – training is the first thing they cut. The contrarian view is that when others aren't doing something, that is the best time for you to do it. If your competition isn't training their leaders, this can be an opportunity for you to create competitive advantage by training yours. Think about it, as your company leadership skills keep getting better, your competition is in a holding pattern. Who do you think will be more successful in the short term and the long term?

Dedicate yourself with passion and commitment – Position and title may give you power but power in itself does not make you an effective leader. To become an effective leader there are specific skill sets that you must understand and master. This does not come naturally. It takes dedication, passion and commitment to the process. That commitment, dedication and passion includes a tireless effort to improve on specific skills and the development of a personal leadership methodology.

Creating competitive advantage – Whenever the economy,

this year or next, starts getting much better, success will come at a much greater pace if you have proactively built leadership skills into the organization. I realize the economic realities may be that you are in a contingency mode and you are forced to make serious cost reductions. But, be careful not to throw the baby out with the bathwater. Remember, companies that will thrive in a tough economic environment are companies that continuously develop leadership skills at every level in the organization. This includes sales management, territory management and even supervisory level employees. **Winning organizations** seem to have a knack for leadership development throughout their organization. One key principle that I have found present in this type of organization is the fact that they hire well and they fire better. Generally their managers have been trained on the interviewing and hiring process. As a result, their success rate for finding and keeping good employees is above average. Recruitment and retention becomes part of their culture and the responsibility of everyone. Leadership is more than just a word in these companies and leadership potential is sought out, encouraged and developed. Every successful leader I have ever known has taken direct responsibility for the development of leadership in others.

True Effective Leadership is a Scarce Commodity

"Rick, I've been with this company twenty years. What's the point in trying all this 21st century leadership mumbo jumbo when the economic sky is falling on us?"

It's never too late to accept the responsibility for your personal leadership development or the development of leadership skills in your subordinates. One of the biggest needs today in the majority of organizations is the unique leadership ability to transform the organization to win in a tough economic environment. This is not just the responsibility of the CEO. Leaders at all levels of the management hierarchy need to develop this type of leadership. Then and only then can an organization create and maintain competitive advantage in tough economic times.

So...... Leadership in Tough Economic Times Requires That You

- **Plan Carefully** - Planning carefully prevents knee jerk decisions. I don't care what you call your plan, strategic, contingency or just business planning. The point is this, if you haven't done any planning beyond what you are going to do for lunch -- now is the time to start. Dealing with tough economic times will require utilization of all your leadership skills and planning is a key skill that is practiced by the most effective leaders.

- **Anticipate Resistance** - Resistance is often a result of fear. Make sure you maintain a positive attitude. Your thoughts are powerful and they set the tone for the organization. Pull your tail from between your legs and look at economic crisis as an opportunity to gain market share and exploit your competition.

- **Communicate Openly and Honestly** - Most resistance is due to lack of information. Most companies under communicate. This can be especially crippling during an economic crisis. If you can't trust your management team enough to be totally open --- then you have the wrong team. Don't ignore the rest of the organization either. Keep everyone informed on a monthly if not a weekly basis. An employee's number one concern during an economic crisis is their security.

- **Employee Buy In** - Get employees involved in the early stages of change. It's the employees that will get you through this crisis. Make no mistake, employees create profitably.

- **Execution** - The golden grail ---- nothing happens unless you execute. Accountability must become a priority. This means follow-up coaching and guidance must be the mantra for all managers. Accountability must be all encompassing including holding the CEO accountable.
- **Trust and Respect Employees -** Credibility based on your past relationships will play a key role in creating success. Employees won't start trusting you until you start trusting them. Employees won't start respecting you until you start respecting them. You must understand "Empowerment" and fight the urge to just delegate without allowing the employee to use their initiative and creativity.
- **Invest in the development** of your management team, executive team and your key employees that you depend on for leadership throughout the organization.

This should be your manner and approach to providing direction, implementing plans and motivating people during economic challenge. If you can train and develop leadership in your employees, your personal leadership effectiveness will improve. But remember, arguably, some people believe *there is no such thing as a "Born Leader" even though every human being has some level of innate leadership characteristics and potential.* You never stop learning, you never stop growing and you should never stop training and developing leadership in others. *That is a key ingredient to succeeding during tough economic times.*

Thanks for Being our Mentor

It Gets Lonely at the Top

XI

Being a President, CEO or the owner of a company can get lonely at times. This is true even if you are an excellent leader and have developed a topnotch executive staff. Often times you face decisions, challenges or just thoughts that you can't even divulge to your most trusted employee. Some CEOs use executive coaches to help them during these times. I personally do some executive coaching. Often times coaching is just affirmation and validation of one's own thinking but it is important to have that outlet.

Other leaders, owners and Presidents use a Board of Directors (BOD) for guidance and consultation. A BOD, elected by ownership, can provide the kind of support necessary to take the company to the next level. No man is an island and it *can* become very lonely at the top especially when you are facing economic turbulence and the potential for contingency planning or restructuring. Growing an organization is hard work. Maintaining profitability in tough economic times is hard work. The president of the corporation not only has to surround himself with an excellent team but he must be able to rely on another power to challenge him and his team. The

BOD, in exercising its business judgment, acts as an advisor and counselor to the President and his executive team. The Board can help define and enforce standards of accountability. A Board can challenge and help the management team execute their responsibilities to the fullest extent in the best interest of the shareholders.

A Sounding Board

A BOD can have differing types of responsibilities based on its written charter and by laws. However, the typical responsibilities that a BOD for a privately held corporation must live up to are generally aligned with ownership/shareholder objectives. Overseeing the way the company conducts its business to ensure that it is managed effectively is one primary responsibility. Selecting, compensating and evaluating the CEO is another key responsibility. Someone has to have the power to take the CEO to the woodshed when it becomes necessary. No one person has all the answers and the Board can provide the kind of advice and insight that may circumvent mistakes or validate the direction the CEO is taking the company in.

Structure

Boards can be structured under a wide range of responsibilities and personalities. They can be very formal with strict procedural requirements or they can be very informal, made up of predominantly family members without the necessity of following "Roberts Rules of Order" in conducting its business. It's the opinion of this author that every Board including the "Family Advisory" Board needs to have several outside directors elected. These outside board members are not the company accountant, the company attorney or best buddies with the owners. They are proven successful business people that can serve the BOD in an uncompromising objective manner. The BOD can support management in the development of organizational planning, succession and resource management. The most effective

BOD will be a group of professionals with a wide variety of skills. Ideally, these board members will have backgrounds that differ from the management team but compliment their skill sets.

The Board Personality

Just like management, a Board of Directors' success and how supportive it is to management is directly related to their personality traits and their character. Selecting directors for board membership is critical and the process should not be taken lightly. These directors must perform the role of governance, although their primary role is one of a supporter, a coach and even mentors. They must also assume the role of questioners and monitors of company performance. As supporters they must provide guidance and advice while living up to their governance responsibility which ensures the long term health of the organization. This role includes succession planning and holding the CEO and the management team accountable for the success of the organization. That is why the director's character is so important. A character that embraces the following:

- Honesty
- Integrity
- Enthusiasm
- Open mindedness
- Competence
- Trustworthiness
- Analytical thinking
- Being a team player
- A sense of humor

The executive team should create the roadmap, develop the plan and the BOD will review and approve it. Monitoring the company's financial performance, reporting policies and accounting practices are part of this process. Compliance and risk management also become a part of the Board's responsibilities.

So What Does the Management Team Do?

It sounds like the management team will spend most of it's time trying to keep the Board happy. Not true. The role of the CEO and the management team is quite clear. They run the company. The company's day-to-day business will always remain the responsibility of its employees under the direction of senior management and the CEO. The CEO is held accountable, as he should be, by the Board of Directors. Once the management team creates the strategic plan and it is approved by the Board, they are fully empowered to execute the plan.

Role of the Director

Directors are expected to demonstrate the kind of character that is beyond reproach. They must always act in the best interests of the business and fulfill their fiduciary responsibilities. They must always act honestly, ethically and with integrity. They must always maintain a courteous and respectful attitude. They will act in good faith exercising sound judgment, competence and due diligence. They must maintain the confidentiality of the organization and avoid any conflict of interests. Being a director should never be taken lightly. It requires time, attention and dedication. They are expected to attend all the scheduled meetings and serve on necessary committees that are in the best interest of the organization.

A BOD should not perform an adversarial role but a supportive role to the CEO and the management team of the organization. The right board members can be significant part of the success of the organization. The power the board has is dependent upon its charter and its bylaws. Remember, the board is elected by the shareholders. In a privately held corporation, this means that ownership determines the makeup and type of board they want to govern the organization. Successful owners, true leaders understand the value a board of directors can provide.

Final Thoughts

Let's face it --- *"The Economy Sucks."* And, being in a recession is not something many of us have experienced before. Simply put, there are good times when things are going well and it's easy to make money, and there are bad times, when it's much more difficult to make money. Prior to the recession starting, we had enjoyed an extended period of exceptionally good business conditions. Revenue and profits exceeded most of our expectations. During these times leadership and success often came much easier than it should have. Too much good can often dull the edge necessary to excel in tougher times.

Leadership is brutally tested by economic challenge. If you aren't prepared, if you have no plan, things can become extremely difficult. Planning carefully prevents knee jerk decisions. The point is this, if you haven't done any planning beyond what you are going to do for lunch -- now is the time to start. Tough economic times require utilization of all your leadership skills and planning is a key skill that is practiced by the most effective leaders.

My Focus is Surviving this Recession

Of course you have to look at the short term and get through this economic crisis. But, don't make the mistake of ignoring the development of your long term strategic plan. We have faced recessions before and we have always come out of them stronger than before. We can and will do it again. We can as a country based on our free enterprise system. You need to be prepared to take advantage of the opportunities that will present themselves as economic conditions begin to improve. That means you and your team must have a "Vision for the Future." As I mentioned earlier I call it an "End Game" that becomes the platform for the development of your strategic plan.

Doing business today is just not as easy as it was when we were riding the high wave of the economic boom. You are actually going to have to know what you are doing to get through this economic crisis. That means you have to dust off your visionary skills. Often, these skills take a back seat when our attitude leans more toward survival.

Recessionary Leadership Development

When you are in the midst of a tough economy, a recession, this can make it convenient if not easy to ignore your responsibilities as leaders to invest and develop employees within your organization. Sure times are tough. Recently I had a CEO say to me:

"Rick, what happens if we continue to invest in leadership development and the employee leaves?"

My answer was simple, although I can't take credit for it since I heard the answer at a seminar years ago.

"Jim," I replied, "What if you don't invest in their development and they stay?"

Listen, times are tough. Some of you may even be facing economic crisis. Keep in mind that as a leader you don't create crisis. But, a crisis can create leaders. Now is the time to leverage the current economic crisis to enhance leadership development within your company. Ask yourself these questions:

- What kind of example are you setting during these tough economic times? The majority of your employees have probably never experienced a recession.
- What kind of knowledge or experience are you passing down?
- Are you living up to your responsibility to have a personal impact on leadership development within the organization?
- What kind of mentor have you been?
- Are you allowing your employees to stretch – to fail – to grow?
- Are you empowering and demonstrating faith and trust in your employees?

Leadership Responsibility

The key to being an effective leader is the ability to influence the influencers. You have to touch people in such a way that they can reach out and touch other people. You alone will not maximize success during this recession. It takes an entire team. However, it's up to you to make sure you have developed that team to reach their personal maximum potential. Leadership isn't something you learn from a book or a college course. It is developed over time. You can't inject it into an employee but you can enhance their leadership skills through your personal guidance and mentoring. Inspire greatness in others is a phrase often used to define leadership responsibility. This isn't the easiest challenge you will ever face. Potential leaders need time to learn from their own failures; to comprehend consequences and develop scar tissue. Correction is not rejection and constructive feedback is an effective coaching tool. If you suddenly have an epiphany and decide you should become a mentor and start developing your team, go for it --- it's never too late. However, if you have been cognizant of the need for leadership and have invested in employee development, you already have an advantage over many of your competitors. Now is the time to leverage that advantage.

Leveraging Development

Potential leaders are recognized as already having the basic tools. These tools include intelligence, integrity, character and a moral value system for doing the right thing. The rest of the formula can be developed. That formula includes the ability to become a strategic thinker. Creating a vision that deals with the future as well as the present considering both internal and external challenges. One of the most critical skills that need to be developed is the ability to recognize talent in others. This skill set also requires the intuitive mindset to recognize poor performance and the ability to weed out those that cannot meet the challenges necessary to maximize success. *"Weed the Garden" before the flowers become overgrown with poor performance and resentment...*

As a leader you cannot afford to allow your organization to experience a leadership vacuum during economic turmoil. As a leader you are called upon to make unpleasant decisions during these economic times. You may face unpalatable choices. However, those employees that remain committed to the company's success will recognize and respect the necessity for those decisions as long as you are fair and consistent in your actions. It requires courage and a strong stomach. The job that leaders have is difficult and there are increasingly fewer people capable of doing it. That makes it even more important that you continue investing in leadership development.

The absolutely best way to maximize your company's success is to have people working for you that are better than you are; people that compliment your strengths and negate your personal weaknesses. This is impossible if you can't set your ego aside and realize that developing talent in other people makes you personally a much more effective leader. Having that kind of emotional self-confidence is vital to leaders. You and your company will never become perfect. But, you can be passionately committed to pursuing excellence.

Mentoring

"Becoming a confidant—leading through the use of past examples and experiences."

After all, mentoring is providing guidance, support and training to expedite the development of someone who has the potential to become an effective leader. And consequently, mentoring helps define one's purpose, values, skills and unique talents. In reality, actual experiences and what's learned from those experiences is a key part of the learning process. Mentoring is also essential to this experienced based learning. There aren't many successful people in life who haven't had the help of someone along the way. That help may have appeared in the form of a role model, the support of a particular group, a personal friend and confidant or a hands-on mentor.

Mentoring involves commitment and a long-term relationship that an experienced leader makes to support the professional development of a protégé. This relationship can be a formal or an informal process. However, since this process is so valuable, many companies look for ways to create formal mentoring programs. The bottom line is that it's really all about leadership development. Mentoring can take the form of challenging assignments that create unique opportunities to gain experience in specific leadership areas.

Plan Success --- Not Failure

These days it seems the message being sent to everyone is how to survive in this turbulent economy. If you are a true leader you are looking for ways to thrive. It's hard to escape the news of economic downturns; lay-offs, and stock market fluctuations. It's what you do with that information that will set you apart from the rest. If you're a person that allows this kind of information to affect your daily thinking and decision making, it's time for you to turn off the TV and turn on your creative mindset. **Get tuned into the solutions and stop focusing on the problems.**

An economic downturn is not the end all be all, in fact all it means is things are changing. Solution based thinking is a principle leadership skill. It's time to leverage your leadership skills and the leadership skills you continue to develop in your management team. Get ahead of the game and don't allow your company to be a victim of it.

If your mindset is simply the desire to just survive this economic cycle and you are hoping you can outlast the storm, *you are actually planning for failure*. Your mindset will become the mindset of your team. You are the leader. Your thoughts are powerful. They will show through any kind of front you may display. Times are tough but the sky isn't falling. So start thinking and acting in such a way that you can gain market share in any economic climate. You want to thrive not just survive. Live up to your responsibilities of being the leader and focus on the development of leadership throughout your organization. Leadership creates success. You will be amazed at what you can accomplish if you have surrounded yourself with real leadership potential and you and your team actively seeks leadership development as a core competence.

This book deals with contingency planning and restructuring a Turn-A Round. Fixing the problem requires high impact leadership to identify and eliminate the factors that could lead the company to the brink of financial disaster during economic turbulent times.

Throughout the chapters in this book we have discussed changing cost structures, improving asset utilizations and making operational changes. We discussed the process of analyzing operations, economics, cash flow dynamics and strategic planning. However, we must not ignore the fact that contingency planning or restructuring cannot succeed in any organization without the revitalization of its people. And, revitalization of the people requires high impact leadership. Contingency planning and restructuring is an intensive short-term intervention. Revitalization is the key to long term success for the organization.

A company finding itself in difficult situation due to economic financial distress requires rapid analysis, quick decisions and immediate actions. This is undertaken with a deep sense of urgency.

Oftentimes, the reason a company finds itself in financial distress is not the result of economic conditions alone. The economy may just bring the real issues and challenges to the surface. Problems may be traced directly back to the executive staff and past management practices. This becomes the platform for discovery of "The Real Deal." As described in earlier chapters, there may be ownership issues. The president or one or more of the executive staff may be at the core of the problem. This needs to be determined quickly and resolved with minimal compassion and maximum concern for the company's survival.

Success Isn't a Mystery in any Economy

My first piece of advice on success today for anyone willing to listen is simply to turn off the news. Don't listen to CNN. Turn off the Fox News network, NBC, CNBC and all the other networks that are sensationalizing everything that is happening in our economy on a minute to minute basis. I have made a conscious decision not to listen because a high percentage of what you see on television today is pure garbage designed simply to improve ratings. I refuse to listen to a constant diet of negativity. In fact, I refuse to even associate with negative people. I suggest that each and every one of us has an obligation to protect our attitude.

Visualization is Powerful

Ask Tiger Woods or any other professional athlete for that matter about visualization. If you visualize failure, in effect, you can create your own failure. It becomes a self-fulfilling prophecy. By the same token, the "Law of Attraction" also works. If you visualize success you increase your chances of creating success. This isn't some mystic power from the universe. It's actually quite simple. Your thoughts control your behaviors. If you visualize positive things your behaviors are more likely to be positive. You will view things differently, recognize opportunities much quicker and actually generate creative ideas to act upon. Those actions then drive your success.

The Top 5 – 10% of the Success Chain

It is often said that it is the top five to ten percent of the wealthy that create jobs for the rest of the country. That isn't mystical either. It is simply a basic principle of the free enterprise system. The majority of employees today, undervalue their own abilities and become protective of what they have. This puts them in a low risk defensive mentality that inhibits their creativity and willingness to take any kind of risk. This mentality is probably why research has suggested that only 20% of all employees actually reach their own personal potential.

So.... Let's start there. That statistic says that there is tremendous opportunity for the majority of employees to increase their chance of realizing their full potential. No matter what situation you find yourself in, make a pledge right now that no matter how tough the journey seems, you are committed, and you will not give up. You will maximize your own personal potential and the potential of your employees. It starts with taking responsibility for who you were, who you are, but more importantly – who you want to become. Let go of your fears. Change is scary but if you create it, you can control it. Be a little bit of a maverick. Decide to take some calculated risk. Begin to look at all your options.

Maximize Performance through Understanding

To be effective, leaders must not only manage their team, but they must develop an understanding of every individual on that team. Prioritizing acquainting yourself with each individual on your team includes knowing their dreams, their hopes, their thoughts, their opinions and their values. This and only this is the key to making sure you not only have the right team in place, but it enhances your ability as a leader to maximize performance.

The most effective leaders seem to have both a unique ability to pick the right people for their team, but they are superior in reading and understanding people. Getting to know and understand people really doesn't take an enormous amount of time or effort for effective leaders. I often perform business assessments and one of the most effective tools in determining the challenges facing the business is simply meeting with individual employees for an hour or less and listening to them. I mean really listening. It is amazing what employees will tell you by asking a few precise questions and having the discipline to then shut up and listen.

Understanding is Paramount to Success

Understanding the leaders you have selected for your team is paramount to the success of the business. That means you must ask questions that go beyond the business itself. The right questions reveal passions, beliefs and values. Questions like:

- What are your long term goals – dreams?
- What brings a tear to your eyes?
- What is your biggest passion in life?
- What has been the biggest tragedy in your life?
- What has been the biggest joy in your life?

Keep in mind, your discussions with your team members are not an interrogation. These questions may be asked over an expanded time period but you need to have a deep understanding of every team member you have surrounded yourself with. Your effectiveness as a leader and your success as a business depend on it.

Your discussions should reveal their passions; a light should brighten in their eyes and an excitement should overtake the conversation. An effective leader must be able to interact with employees, peers, superiors and many other individuals both inside and outside the organization. But, the most important relationship they must nurture is the relationship with the leadership team they have surrounded themselves with. This team must gain the support of many people to meet or exceed established objectives. This means that they must develop or possess a unique understanding of people. The ability to coach-mentor and teach leadership skills to others is the driving force that will create a winning organization. To do this requires a passion for success. That means understanding the individual passions of your team. Being an effective leader requires the understanding of the principles that govern employee behavior. Accomplish that and success is imminent.

Women in Leadership— This Countries Most Under Utilized Asset

In the spirit of full disclosure, I must admit that I am definitely a card carrying member of the Baby Boomers. I also admit that during my early career in the 70's, I could have undoubtedly been considered a poster child for the "Male Chauvinistic Pig" movement. However, experience and maturity have taught me a great lesson regarding leadership and the abilities, intelligence and values of the female employee. Today, I firmly believe that women in the workplace are the most underutilized asset this country has. Women have led companies and our currently leading companies during tough economic times and they are successful at it.

We have come a long way from that chauvinistic attitude of the past that believed men are simply better, more natural leaders; the belief that women's careers were compromised by their responsibilities at home. Yes we have come a long way. But, statistics are still shocking for women who hope to succeed in the business world.

Today, women occupy 40% of all managerial positions in the United States but only 6% of the *Fortune* 500's top executives are female. (Newsweek Magazine)

What a Chauvinistic Pig!

In your industry this percentage may even be lower. The "glass ceiling," or the idea that women successfully climb the corporate ladder until they're blocked by this transparent ceiling, has been accepted as the largest obstacle to female leadership in the workplace. Hillary Clinton and Sarah Palin claimed to have put millions of cracks in this ceiling but it hasn't been completely shattered yet.

This ceiling represents many characteristics that even most men would challenge and yet they still exist. There are barriers that limit industry's ability to capitalize on the enormous amount of leadership potential that exits in almost any work place in this country. Barriers that women encounter at all levels include prejudicial resistance to women's leadership, leadership style issues and family demands. These obstacles may even create an uneasy feeling for women or their relationship with leadership and the power it commands. A few female leaders have told me that they fear that the power of leadership can give off the impression that they are ruthless or pushy. These are issues that challenge their basic character and femininity; challenges that men don't have to encounter.

Diversity is Strength

Companies that recognize the female leadership talent pool that exists within the confines of their own office will implement specific initiatives to leverage that talent. One of the very basic and first steps to recognizing this talent is to begin evaluating the female employee based on specific contributions as opposed to hours worked. Creating work teams, project teams and management teams that include more than one lone female allows that talent to grow and prosper instead of being suppressed by male domination. Closing the leadership gap and leveraging this talent has to become a priority for businesses of all nature if we are to remain competitive in the global environment. For this country to have this much inherent talent and yet very few women in the top levels of the chain of command is disturbing.

But Women Have Babies

So What!! The idea that women having babies need broader support and special handling is simply hog wash. Women that strive to be leaders and want to contribute at a higher level of hierarchy are often more capable of managing a life balance than most men. And yet, experts have stated that the average lifetime earnings of a highly-skilled female leader who has a child in her twenties is $625,000; while the average lifetime earnings for those having a baby in their thirties is $750,000. For those who have no babies, lifetime earnings reach $913,000." Does that sound discriminatory?

Women in Business Have Been Stereotyped

Rachael Roy, a top designer and CEO of her own company stated that *"Many young women apply self worth to the attention they receive from men. This type of attention is instantly gratifying."*

It's a good thing we are married. Otherwise, you'd be guilty of sexual harassment!

This is unfortunate because this type of gratification contributes to the stereotype and inhibits leadership confidence and leadership integrity. This is social conditioning. There is no more important skill in attaining success than your ability to communicate effectively. Yet women are often sabotaged by their communication skills. Differences in how men and women communicate are rooted in social conditioning. Stereotyped behavior has been expected of women since time began. Women are not expected to argue, displaying anger. Women are expected to be polite in the workplace and not curse. They are expected to be cooperative and, by and large, docile.

It Starts with Effective Communication

Effective communication with your leadership team is the breath of life, the first spark to ignite success. Nothing else is so crucial to survival, solidarity and the ability to grow market share. True leaders inspire others to greatness. Inspiring your team starts by taking that first step to really understand who they are, what they are about and the principles they stand for. Effective face to face communication is your platform to provide that inspiration.

Men Have Different Rules

The same rules or expectations do not apply to men. Women have always been encouraged to speak softly and smile a lot and yet men are not chastised for emotional outbursts most of the time. This gender differentiation begins early in life. Men in the business world generally have few, if any, qualms about issuing orders or voicing complaints. Many women tend to be uncomfortable pulling rank; they seek agreement and consistency. Disagreement and conflict don't affect men in the same way; some even enjoy it, while women typically go out of their way to avoid confrontation.

Men expect and are expected to be successful. We certainly are willing to take full credit when we do succeed. The principle for success on the part of women is different. Many women only hope to be successful. When women do succeed they are more apt to demonstrate true leadership character by attributing their success to teamwork or the support of their peers and subordinates.

Women Do Have Power

Traditionally, in the business world, the male model of authority was considered superior to the female model of collaboration. However, it's becoming abundantly clear that effective communication is the essence of good leadership and that is what really counts. Either style can be effective based on

Please – You don't have to BEG!

ones individual leadership model. The key to success lies in focusing on and creating for one's self a style that encompasses the best of both authority and collaboration with an emphasis on a servant style of leadership.

Women as a group can be very powerful if they would only embrace that power. They must reject in disbelief that business is strictly a man's world and that they must follow man's rule. Women have different values, different styles and different approaches to many things. Men could be well served to listen more. We must leverage every asset we have to maximize success. Women may not have all the answers but I submit they may have many that we as men haven't realized yet.

So, as you review your employee development plans, don't ignore the potential that may exist at the receptionist desk, customer service or accounting where you traditionally find many of your female employees. Search for leadership potential regardless of gender and you may find a number of diamonds in the rough.

It's Your Responsibility

Understanding the team you have put in place, whether you are male or female, to help you run the company is not a luxury. It is a responsibility you must accept as a leader. Every one of us is a human being with different values, different beliefs, different back rounds and different views. Ask yourself, "how can I possibly be an effective leader without a complete understanding of every one of my team members?"

Remember, one person can't turn a company around. Organizational charts don't turn companies around; short-term plans, strategic initiatives and restructuring don't turn companies around. People turn companies around. People that believe; people that are committed; people who care and people with values turn companies around. You don't find people with these traits in an organization that doesn't demonstrate high impact executive leadership.

I hope you enjoyed reading "Stop the Bleeding". Visit our website www.ceostrategist.com and sign up for our monthly newsletter – "The Howl".

About the Author

Dr. Eric (Rick) Johnson Biography

Rick Johnson has over 35 years of experience in distribution sales and operations. Rick's career can be broken down by decades. The **first ten years** of his distribution career were spent with the largest steel-processing distributor in the world (Joseph T. Ryerson).

The **second ten years** began with Rick starting his own processing distribution center from scratch. In the first year, sales reached $1 million dollars and had grown to $25 million in its tenth year when Rick sold the business to one of the major national chains.

The **third ten years** of Rick's career dealing with financially troubled Turn-A-Round companies.

After completing ten years of TAR work, Rick decided a decade of acting like Darth Vader was enough and became a consultant to the Wholesale Distribution Industry in 1999.

Rick received an MBA from Keller Graduate School in Chicago and a Bachelor's degree from Capital University, Columbus Ohio. He also served in the United States Air Force. Rick completed his dissertation on Strategic Leadership and received his Ph.D. in 2005. Rick is frequently published in *numerous magazines including a column in Supply House Times*, with over 250 different articles published to date. He's also a published author with eight other books to his credit including:

1. Lone Wolf to Lead Wolf the Evolution of Sales
2. Model Driven Leadership for the 21st Century
3. The Tool Kit for Wholesale Distribution (NAW)
4. The Roadmap
5. Shattered Innocents – (Fiction Novel)
6. Turning Lone Wolves into Lead Wolves – 56 Ideas to Maximize Sales
7. The Lead Wolf Pocket Guide to Leadership
8. Profit is NOT a Dirty Word

LaVergne, TN USA
04 December 2009

166036LV00002B/4/P

9 781432 746179